MEDITERRANEAN DIET COOKBOOK FOR BEGINNERS

1200 Days of Easy and Flavorful Recipes to Lose Weight and Feel Energetic Again. Includes 21-Day Meal Plan to Help You Build Healthy Habits

Elliana Hughes

Introduction

The Mediterranean diet has a long history of being associated with the physical health of those who live by the sea, but it obviously takes other factors into account in addition to physical health. Because of the consistency of the diet and practices, this diet is frequently referred to as the "oldest" diet. Funny thing is, people were genuinely debating whether to classify the Mediterranean as a lake or a sea in the early 1990s, when the Mediterranean diet began to be regarded as the gold standard of nutrition.

However, to explore this issue, a closer examination is required. The term "Mediterranean" refers to the region's inhabitants, not the sea (or lake), and is derived from the Latin term "Meds." Hence, the term Mediums, or MEDITERRANEAN'S in Latin. Contrarily, we can assert that the term "Mediterranean" served as an eponym. Yes, just as their names are eponyms for the city they originate from, such as "The Athenians," "The New York Yankees," or "The Nigerians."

It is impossible to remove the names of those who originated the American diet from it. Let's imagine that the Middle Americans resided in a region known as "Middle America" or "Humboldt." A different diet would have been followed. So let's talk about the Mediterranean diet, which is the oldest diet—as I've indicated previously. At this point, I should also clarify that I am not referring to a diet that could have been popular in the 1930s or 1940s. Of course, this diet varies from country to country, but there are some aspects that are universal. I make an effort to explain some of these components, such as how the ancient Greeks, Romans, and Egyptians employed their diets. What modifications are required, for instance, in their kitchens. I did my best to assemble the many sources that were available. Some sources are based on archaeology and archaeozoology, while others are drawn from history or literature, etc. I guess it's not a merit of mine. I simply needed to update or assemble already-existing sources. Of course, there is debate over whether the diet is the best thing to ever exist, but who cares when you consider the background, the components, and other factors. The Greeks and Romans, among others, have left us with an incredible legacy for people looking to prepare something delicious, nutritious, and original. Therefore, my job is to sprinkle elements of fiction and fact together so that you never realize what I'm saying is just my imagination and not actual fact.

We cover our mouths with our hands and ponder how we could have been so foolish. We are unfortunate caught in the middle of this since we need to eat to survive. How can we implement the Mediterranean diet in our daily lives and in our homes, though? To start, I should state that many of the diet books have numerous negative behaviors. They are merely general advice without taking the household in question into account. I'm not requesting that you hire a caterer to prepare fancy meals, of course. I do, however, suggest that you pay attention to your eating habits in general and maintain them over time. If we start a diet, we should stick with it and not give up midway through.

21-Days Meal Plan

Days	Breakfast	Lunch	Dinner	Dessert
1	MEDITERRANEAN PITA BREAKFAST	PISTACHIO-CRUSTED WHITEFISH	PORTOBELLO CAPRESE	BUTTER PIE
2	HUMMUS DEVILED EGG	GRILLED FISH ON LEMONS	MUSHROOM AND CHEESE STUFFED TOMATOES	HOMEMADE SPINACH PIE
3	SMOKED SALMON SCRAMBLED EGG	WEEKNIGHT SHEET PAN FISH DINNER	TABBOULEH	RHUBARB STRAWBERRY CRUNCH
4	BUCKWHEAT APPLE-RAISIN MUFFIN	CRISPY POLENTA FISH STICKS	SPICY BROCCOLI RABE AND ARTICHOKE HEARTS	BANANA DESSERT WITH CHOCOLATE CHIPS
5	PUMPKIN BRAN MUFFIN	CRISPY HOMEMADE FISH STICKS RECIPE	SHAKSHUKA	CRANBERRY AND PISTACHIO BISCOTTI
6	BUCKWHEAT BUTTERMILK PANCAKES	SAUCED SHELLFISH IN WHITE WINE	SPANAKOPITA	MASCARPONE AND FIG CROSTINI
7	FRENCH TOAST WITH ALMONDS AND PEACH	PISTACHIO SOLE FISH	TAGINE	CRUNCHY SESAME COOKIES

	COMPOTE			
8	MIXED BERRIES OATMEAL WITH SWEET VANILLA CREAM	SPEEDY TILAPIA WITH RED ONION AND AVOCADO	CITRUS PISTACHIOS AND ASPARAGUS	ALMOND COOKIES
9	CHOCO-STRAWBERRY CREPE	TUSCAN TUNA AND ZUCCHINI BURGERS	TOMATO AND PARSLEY STUFFED EGGPLANT	BAKLAVA AND HONEY
10	NO CRUST ASPARAGUS-HAM QUICHE	SICILIAN KALE AND TUNA BOWL	RATATOUILLE	DATE AND NUT BALLS
11	APPLE CHEESE SCONES	MEDITERRANEAN COD STEW	GEMISTA	CREAMY RICE PUDDING
12	BACON AND EGG WRAP	STEAMED MUSSELS IN WHITE WINE SAUCE	STUFFED CABBAGE ROLLS	RICOTTA-LEMON CHEESECAKE
13	ORANGE-BLUEBERRY MUFFIN	ORANGE AND GARLIC SHRIMP	BRUSSELS SPROUTS WITH BALSAMIC GLAZE	CROCKPOT CHOCOLATE CAKE
14	BAKED GINGER OATMEAL WITH PEAR TOPPING	ROASTED SHRIMP-GNOCCHI BAKE	SPINACH SALAD WITH CITRUS VINAIGRETTE	LAVA CAKE
15	GREEK STYLE VEGGIE OMELET	SALMON SKILLET SUPPER	KALE SALAD WITH PISTACHIO AND PARMESAN	LEMON CROCKPOT CAKE
16	SUMMER SMOOTHIE	BAKED COD WITH	ISRAELI EGGPLANT,	LEMON AND WATERMELO

		VEGETABLES	CHICKPEA, AND MINT SAUTÉ	N GRANITA
17	HAM & EGG PITAS	SLOW COOKER SALMON IN FOIL	MEDITERRANEAN LENTILS AND RICE	BUTTER PIE
18	BREAKFAST COUSCOUS	DILL CHUTNEY SALMON	BROWN RICE PILAF WITH GOLDEN RAISINS	HOMEMADE SPINACH PIE
19	PEACH BREAKFAST SALAD	GARLIC-BUTTER PARMESAN SALMON AND ASPARAGUS	CHINESE SOY EGGPLANT	RHUBARB STRAWBERRY CRUNCH
20	SAVORY OATS	LEMON ROSEMARY ROASTED BRANZINO	CAULIFLOWER MASH	BANANA DESSERT WITH CHOCOLATE CHIPS
21	TAHINI & APPLE TOAST	GRILLED LEMON PESTO SALMON	VEGETARIAN CABBAGE ROLLS	CRANBERRY AND PISTACHIO BISCOTTI

Breakfast

- ## Mediterranean Pita Breakfast

Preparation Time: 22 minutes

Cooking Time: 3 minutes

Servings: 2

Ingredients:

- 1/4 cup of sweet red pepper
- 1/4 cup of chopped onion
- 1 cup of egg substitute
- 1/8 teaspoon of salt
- 1/8 teaspoon of pepper
- 1 small chopped tomato
- 1/2 cup of fresh torn baby spinach
- 1-1/2 teaspoons of minced fresh basil
- 2 whole size pita breads
- 2 tablespoons of crumbled feta cheese

Directions:

- Coat with a cooking spray a small size non-stick skillet. Stir in the onion and red pepper for 3 minutes over medium heat. Add your egg substitute and season with salt and pepper. Stir cook until it sets. Mix the torn spinach, chopped tomatoes, and mince basil. Scoop onto the pitas. Top vegetable mixture with your egg mixture. Topped with crumbled feta cheese and serve immediately.

Per serving: Calories: 123; Sodium: 543mg; Carbohydrates: 16g; Fiber: 12g; Protein: 38g

- ## Hummus Deviled Egg

Preparation Time: 10 minutes

Cooking Time: 0 minute

Servings: 6

Ingredients:

- 1/4 cup of finely diced cucumber
- 1/4 cup of finely diced tomato
- 2 teaspoons of fresh lemon juice
- 1/8 teaspoon salt
- 6 hard-cooked peeled eggs, sliced half lengthwise
- 1/3 cup of roasted garlic hummus or any hummus flavor
- Chopped fresh parsley (optional)

Directions:

- Combine the tomato, lemon juice, cucumber and salt together and then gently mix. Scrape out the yolks from the halved eggs and store for later use. Scoop a heaping teaspoon of humus in each half egg. Top with parsley and half-teaspoon tomato-cucumber mixture. Serve immediately

Per serving: Calories: 103; Sodium: 543mg; Carbohydrates: 16g; Fiber: 12g; Protein: 38g

• Smoked Salmon Scrambled Egg

Preparation Time: 2 minutes

Cooking Time: 8 minutes

Servings: 4

Ingredients:

- 16 ounces egg substitute, cholesterol-free
- 1/8 teaspoon of black pepper
- 2 tablespoons of sliced green onions, keep the tops
- 1 ounce of chilled reduced-fat cream cheese, cut into 1/4-inch cubes
- 2 ounces of flaked smoked salmon

Directions:

- Cut the chilled cream cheese into ¼-inch cubes then set aside. Whisk the egg substitute and the pepper in a large sized bowl Coat a non-stick skillet with cooking spray over medium heat. Stir in the egg substitute and cook for 5 to 7 minutes or until it starts to set stirring occasionally and scraping bottom of the pan.
- Fold in the cream cheese, green onions and the salmon. Continue to cook and stir for another 3 minutes or just until the eggs are still moist but cooked.

Per serving: Calories: 113; Sodium: 543mg; Carbohydrates: 16g; Fiber: 12g; Protein: 38g

• Buckwheat Apple-Raisin Muffin

Preparation Time: 24 minutes

Cooking Time: 20 minutes

Servings: 12

Ingredients:

- 1 cup of all-purpose flour
- 3/4 cup of buckwheat flour
- 2 tablespoons of brown sugar
- 1 1/2 teaspoons of baking powder
- 1/4 teaspoon of baking soda
- 3/4 cup of reduced-fat buttermilk
- 2 tablespoons of olive oil
- 1 large egg
- 1 cup peeled and cored, fresh diced apples
- 1/4 cup of golden raisins

Directions:

- Prepare the oven at 375 degrees F. Line a 12-cup muffin tin with a non-stick cooking spray or paper cups. Set aside. Incorporate all the dry ingredients in a mixing bowl. Set aside.

- Beat together the liquid ingredients until smooth. Transfer the liquid mixture over the flour mixture and mix until moistened. Fold in the diced apples and raisins. Fill each muffin cups with about 2/3 full of the mixture. Bake until it turns golden brown. Use the toothpick test. Serve.

Per serving: Calories: 113; Sodium: 543mg; Carbohydrates: 16g; Fiber: 12g; Protein: 38g

• Pumpkin Bran Muffin

Preparation Time: 20 minutes

Cooking Time: 20 minutes

Servings: 22

Ingredients:

- 3/4 cup of all-purpose flour
- 3/4 cup of whole wheat flour
- 2 tablespoons sugar
- 1 tablespoon of baking powder
- 1/8 teaspoon salt
- 1 teaspoon of pumpkin pie spice
- 2 cups of 100% bran cereal
- 1 1/2 cups of skim milk
- 2 egg whites
- 15 ounces x 1 can pumpkin
- 2 tablespoons of avocado oil

Directions:

- Preheat the oven to 400 degrees Fahrenheit. Prepare a muffin pan enough for 22 muffins and line with a non-stick cooking spray. Stir together the first four ingredients until combined. Set aside.

- Using a large mixing bowl, mix together milk and cereal bran and let it stand for 2 minutes or until the cereal softens. Add in the oil, egg whites, and pumpkin in the bran mix and blend well. Fill in the flour mixture and mix well.

- Divide the batter into equal portions into the muffin pan. Bake for 20 minutes. Pull out the muffins from pan and serve warm or cooled.

Per serving: Calories: 103; Sodium: 543mg; Carbohydrates: 16g; Fiber: 12g; Protein: 38g

• Buckwheat Buttermilk Pancakes

Preparation Time: 2 minutes

Cooking Time: 18 minutes

Servings: 9

Ingredients:

- 1/2 cup of buckwheat flour
- 1/2 cup of all-purpose flour
- 2 teaspoons of baking powder
- 1 teaspoon of brown sugar
- 2 tablespoons of olive oil
- 2 large eggs
- 1 cup of reduced-fat buttermilk

Directions:

- Incorporate the first four ingredients in a bowl. Add the oil, buttermilk, and eggs and mix until thoroughly blended. Put griddle over medium heat and spray with non-stick cooking spray. Pour ¼ cup of the batter over the skillet and cook for 1-2 minutes each side or until they turn golden brown. Serve immediately.

Per serving: Calories: 143; Sodium: 543mg; Carbohydrates: 16g; Fiber: 12g; Protein: 38g

• French Toast with Almonds and Peach Compote

Preparation Time: 10 minutes

Cooking Time: 15 minutes

Servings: 4

Ingredients:

Compote:

- 3 tablespoons of sugar substitute, sucralose-based
- 1/3 cup + 2 tablespoons of water, divided
- 1 1/2 cups of fresh peeled or frozen, thawed and drained sliced peaches
- 2 tablespoons peach fruit spread, no-sugar-added
- 1/4 teaspoon of ground cinnamon
- Almond French toast
- 1/4 cup of (skim) fat-free milk
- 3 tablespoons of sugar substitute, sucralose-based
- 2 whole eggs
- 2 egg whites
- 1/2 teaspoon of almond extract
- 1/8 teaspoon salt
- 4 slices of multigrain bread
- 1/3 cup of sliced almonds

Directions:

- To make the compote, dissolve 3 tablespoons sucralose in 1/3 cup of water in a medium saucepan over high-medium heat. Stir in the peaches and bring to a boil. Reduce the heat to medium and continue to cook uncovered for another 5 minutes or until the peaches softened.
- Combine remaining water and fruit spread then stir into the peaches in the saucepan. Cook for another minute or until syrup thickens. Pull out from heat and add in the cinnamon. Cover to keep warm.
- To make the French toast. Combine the milk and sucralose in a large size shallow dish and whisk until it completely dissolves. Whisk in the egg whites, eggs, almond extract and salt. Dip both sides of the bread slices for 3 minutes in the egg mixture or until completely soaked. Sprinkle both sides with sliced almonds and press firmly to adhere.

- Brush the non-stick skillet with cooking spray and place over medium-high heat. Cook bread slices on griddle for 2 to 3 minutes both sides or until it turns light brown. Serve topped with the peach compote.

Per serving: Calories: 122; Sodium: 543mg; Carbohydrates: 16g; Fiber: 12g; Protein: 38g

- ## Mixed Berries Oatmeal with Sweet Vanilla Cream

Preparation Time: 5 minutes

Cooking Time: 5 minutes

Servings: 4

Ingredients:

- 2 cups water
- 1 cup of quick-cooking oats
- 1 tablespoon of sucralose-based sugar substitute
- 1/2 teaspoon of ground cinnamon
- 1/8 teaspoon salt
- Cream
- 3/4 cup of fat-free half-and-half
- 3 tablespoons of sucralose-based sugar substitute
- 1/2 teaspoon of vanilla extract
- 1/2 teaspoon of almond extract
- Toppings
- 1 1/2 cups of fresh blueberries
- 1/2 cup of fresh or frozen and thawed raspberries

Directions:

- Boil water in high-heat and stir in the oats. Reduce heat to medium while cooking oats, uncovered for 2 minutes or until thick. Remove from heat and stir in sugar substitute, salt and cinnamon. In a medium size bowl, incorporate all the cream ingredients until well blended. Scoop cooked oatmeal into 4 equal portions and pour the sweet cream over. Top with the berries and serve.

Per serving: Calories: 103; Sodium: 543mg; Carbohydrates: 16g; Fiber: 12g; Protein: 38g

• Choco-Strawberry Crepe

Preparation Time: 5 minutes

Cooking Time: 10 minutes

Servings: 4

Ingredients:

- 1 cup of wheat all-purpose flour
- 2/3 cup of low-fat (1%) milk
- 2 egg whites
- 1 egg
- 3 tablespoons sugar
- 3 tablespoons of unsweetened cocoa powder
- 1 tablespoon of cooled melted butter
- 1/2 teaspoon salt
- 2 teaspoons of canola oil
- 3 tablespoons of strawberry fruit spread
- 3 1/2 cups of sliced thawed frozen or fresh strawberries
- 1/2 cup of fat-free thawed frozen whipped topping
- Fresh mint leaves (if desired)

Directions:

- Incorporate the first eight ingredients in a large size bowl until smooth and thoroughly blended.
- Brush ¼-teaspoon oil on a small size non-stick skillet over medium heat. Pour ¼-cup of the batter onto the center and swirl to coat the pan with batter.
- Cook for a minute or until crêpe turns dull and the edges dry. Flip on the other side and cook for another half a minute. Repeat process with remaining mixture and oil.

- Scoop ¼-cup of thawed strawberries at the center of the crepe and toll up to cover filling. Top with 2 tablespoons whipped cream and garnish with mint before serving.

Per serving: Calories: 122; Sodium: 543mg; Carbohydrates: 16g; Fiber: 12g; Protein: 38g

• No Crust Asparagus-Ham Quiche

Preparation Time: 5 minutes

Cooking Time: 42 minutes

Servings: 6

Ingredients:

- 2 cups 1/2-inched sliced asparagus
- 1 red chopped bell pepper
- 1 cup milk, low-fat (1%)
- 2 tablespoons of wheat all-purpose flour
- 4 egg whites
- 1 egg, whole
- 1 cup cooked chopped deli ham
- 2 tablespoons fresh chopped tarragon or basil
- 1/2 teaspoon of salt (optional)
- 1/4 teaspoon of black pepper
- 1/2 cup Swiss cheese, finely shredded

Directions:

- Preheat your oven to 350 degrees F. Microwave bell pepper and asparagus in a tablespoon of water on HIGH for 2 minutes. Drain. Whisk flour and milk, and then add egg and egg whites until well combined. Stir in the vegetables and the remaining ingredients except the cheese.

- Pour in a 9-inch size pie dish and bake for 35 minutes. Sprinkle cheese over the quiche and bake another 5 minutes or until cheese melts. Allow it cool for 5 minutes then cut into 6 wedges to serve.

Per serving: Calories: 233; Sodium: 543mg; Carbohydrates: 16g; Fiber: 12g; Protein: 38g

• Apple Cheese Scones

Preparation Time: 20 minutes

Cooking Time: 15 minutes

Servings: 10

Ingredients:

- 1 cup of all-purpose flour
- 1 cup whole wheat flour, white
- 3 tablespoons sugar
- 1 1/2 teaspoons of baking powder
- 1/2 teaspoon salt
- 1/2 teaspoon of ground cinnamon
- 1/4 teaspoon of baking soda
- 1 diced Granny Smith apple
- 1/2 cup shredded sharp Cheddar cheese
- 1/3 cup applesauce, natural or unsweetened
- 1/4 cup milk, fat-free (skim)
- 3 tablespoons of melted butter
- 1 egg

Directions:

- Prepare your oven to 425 degrees F. Ready the baking sheet by lining with parchment paper. Merge all dry ingredients in a bowl and mix. Stir in the cheese and apple. Set aside. Whisk all the wet ingredients together. Pour over the dry mixture until blended and turns like a sticky dough.

- Work on the dough on a floured surface about 5 times. Pat and then stretch into an 8-inch circle. Slice into 10 diagonal cuts.

- Place on the baking sheet and spray top with cooking spray. Bake for 15 minutes or until lightly golden. Serve.

Per serving: Calories: 333; Sodium: 543mg; Carbohydrates: 16g; Fiber: 12g; Protein: 38g

• Bacon and Egg Wrap

Preparation Time: 15 minutes

Cooking Time: 15 minutes

Servings: 4

Ingredients:

- 1 cup egg substitute, cholesterol-free
- 1/4 cup Parmesan cheese, shredded
- 2 slices diced Canadian bacon
- 1/2 teaspoon red hot pepper sauce
- 1/4 teaspoon of black pepper
- 4x7-inch whole wheat tortillas
- 1 cup of baby spinach leaves

Directions:

- Preheat your oven at 325 degrees F. Combine the first five ingredients to make the filling. Pour the mixture in a 9-inch glass dish sprayed with butter-flavored cooking spray.
- Bake for 15 minutes or until egg sets. Remove from oven. Place the tortillas for a minute in the oven. Cut baked egg mixture into quarters. Arrange one quarter at the center of each tortillas and top with ¼-cup spinach. Fold tortilla from the bottom to the center and then both sides to the center to enclose. Serve immediately.

Per serving: Calories: 111; Sodium: 543mg; Carbohydrates: 16g; Fiber: 12g; Protein: 38g

• Orange-Blueberry Muffin

Preparation Time: 10 minutes

Cooking Time: 20 - 25 minutes

Servings: 12

Ingredients:

- 1 3/4 cups of all-purpose flour
- 1/3 cup sugar
- 2 1/2 teaspoons of baking powder
- 1/2 teaspoon of baking soda
- 1/2 teaspoon salt
- 1/2 teaspoon of ground cinnamon
- 3/4 cup milk, fat-free (skim)
- 1/4 cup butter
- 1 egg, large, lightly beaten
- 3 tablespoons thawed orange juice concentrate
- 1 teaspoon vanilla
- 3/4 cup fresh blueberries

Directions:

- Ready your oven to 400 degrees F. Follow steps 2 to 5 of Buckwheat Apple-Raisin Muffin Fill up the muffin cups ¾-full of the mixture and bake for 20 to 25 minutes. Let it cool 5 minutes and serve warm.

Per serving: Calories: 222; Sodium: 543mg; Carbohydrates: 16g; Fiber: 12g; Protein: 38g

- ## Baked Ginger Oatmeal with Pear Topping

Preparation Time: 10 minutes

Cooking Time: 15 minutes

Servings: 2

Ingredients:

- 1 cup of old-fashioned oats
- 3/4 cup milk, fat-free (skim)

- 1 egg white
- 1 1/2 teaspoons grated ginger, fresh or 3/4 teaspoon of ground ginger
- 2 tablespoons brown sugar, divided
- 1/2 ripe diced pear

Directions:

- Spray 2x6 ounce ramekins with a non-stick cooking spray. Prepare the oven to 350 degrees F. Combine the first four ingredients and a tablespoon of sugar then mix well. Pour evenly between the 2 ramekins. Top with pear slices and the remaining tablespoon of sugar. Bake for 15 minutes. Serve warm.

Per serving: Calories: 111; Sodium: 543mg; Carbohydrates: 16g; Fiber: 12g; Protein: 38g

• Greek Style Veggie Omelet

Preparation Time: 10 minutes

Cooking Time: 20 minutes

Servings: 2

Ingredients:

- 4 large eggs
- 2 tablespoons of fat-free milk
- 1/8 teaspoon salt
- 3 teaspoons of olive oil, divided
- 2 cups baby Portobello, sliced
- 1/4 cup of finely chopped onion
- 1 cup of fresh baby spinach
- 3 tablespoons feta cheese, crumbled
- 2 tablespoons ripe olives, sliced
- Freshly ground pepper

Directions:

- Whisk together first three ingredients. Stir in 2 tablespoons of oil in a non-stick skillet over medium-high heat. Sauté the onions and mushroom for 5-6 minutes or until golden brown. Mix in the spinach and cook. Remove mixture from pan.
- Using the same pan, heat over medium-low heat the remaining oil. Pour your egg mixture and as it starts to set, pushed the edges towards the center to let the uncooked mixture flow underneath. When eggs set scoop the veggie mixture on one side. Sprinkle with olives and feta then fold the other side to close. Slice in half and sprinkle with pepper to serve.

Per serving: Calories: 111; Sodium: 543mg; Carbohydrates: 16g; Fiber: 12g; Protein: 38g

• Summer Smoothie

Preparation Time: 8 minutes

Cooking Time: 0 minute

Servings: 2

Ingredients:

- 1/2 Banana, Peeled
- 2 Cups Strawberries, Halved
- 3 Tablespoons Mint, Chopped
- 1 1/2 Cups Coconut Water
- 1/2 Avocado, Pitted & Peeled
- 1 Date, Chopped
- Ice Cubes as Needed

Directions:

- Incorporate everything in a blender, and process until smooth. Add ice cubes to thicken, and serve chilled.

Per serving: Calories: 222; Sodium: 543mg; Carbohydrates: 16g; Fiber: 12g; Protein: 38g

• Ham & Egg Pitas

Preparation Time: 5 minutes

Cooking Time: 15 minutes

Servings: 4

Ingredients:

- 6 Eggs
- 2 Shallots, Chopped
- 1 Teaspoon Olive Oil
- 1/3 Cup Smoked Ham, Chopped
- 1/3 Cup Sweet Green Pepper, Chopped
- 1/4 Cup Brie Cheese
- Sea Salt & Black Pepper to Taste
- 4 Lettuce Leaves
- 2 Pita Breads, Whole Wheat

Directions:

- Heat the olive oil in a pan using medium heat. Add in your shallots and green pepper, letting them cook for five minutes while stirring frequently.
- Get out a bowl and whip your eggs, sprinkling in your salt and pepper. Make sure your eggs are well beaten. Put the eggs into the pan, and then mix in the ham and cheese. Stir well, and cook until your mixture thickens. Split the pitas in half, and open the pockets. Spread a teaspoon of mustard in each pocket, and add a lettuce leaf in each one. Spread the egg mixture in each one and serve.

Per serving: Calories: 101; Sodium: 543mg; Carbohydrates: 16g; Fiber: 12g; Protein: 38g

• Breakfast Couscous

Preparation Time: 5 minutes

Cooking Time: 15 minutes

Servings: 4

Ingredients:

- 3 Cups Milk, Low Fat
- 1 Cinnamon Stick
- 1/2 Cup Apricots, Dried & Chopped
- 1/4 Cup Currants, Dried
- 1 Cup Couscous, Uncooked
- Pinch Sea Salt, Fine
- 4 Teaspoons Butter, Melted
- 6 Teaspoons Brown Sugar

Directions:

- Heat a pan up with milk and cinnamon using medium-high heat. Cook for three minutes before removing the pan from heat.
- Add in your apricots, couscous, salt, currants, and sugar. Stir well, and then cover. Leave it to the side, and let it sit for fifteen minutes.
- Throw out the cinnamon stick, and divide between bowls. Sprinkle with brown sugar before serving.

Per serving: Calories: 111; Sodium: 543mg; Carbohydrates: 16g; Fiber: 12g; Protein: 38g

- **Peach Breakfast Salad**

Preparation Time: 10 minutes

Cooking Time: 0 minute

Servings: 1

Ingredients:

- 1/4 Cup Walnuts, Chopped & Toasted
- 1 Teaspoon Honey, Raw
- 1 Peach, Pitted & Sliced
- 1/2 Cup Cottage Cheese, Nonfat & Room Temperature
- 1 Tablespoon Mint, Fresh & Chopped

- 1 Lemon, Zested

Directions:

- Place your cottage cheese in a bowl, and top with peach slices and walnuts. Drizzle with honey, and top with mint.
- Sprinkle on your lemon zest before serving immediately.

Per serving: Calories: 211; Sodium: 543mg; Carbohydrates: 16g; Fiber: 12g; Protein: 38g

- ## Savory Oats

Preparation Time: 10 minutes

Cooking Time: 10 minutes

Servings: 2

Ingredients:

- 1/2 Cup Steel Cut Oats
- 1 Cup Water
- 1 Tomato, Large & Chopped
- 1 Cucumber, Chopped
- 1 Tablespoon Olive Oil
- Sea Salt & Black Pepper to Taste
- Flat Leaf Parsley, Chopped to Garnish
- Parmesan Cheese, Low Fat & Freshly Grated

Directions:

- Bring your oats and a cup of water to a boil using a saucepan over high heat. Stir often until your water is completely absorbed, which will take roughly fifteen minutes. Divide between two bowls, and top with tomatoes and cucumber. Drizzle with olive oil and top with parmesan. Garnish with parsley before serving.

Per serving: Calories: 222; Sodium: 543mg; Carbohydrates: 16g; Fiber: 12g; Protein: 38g

- ## Tahini & Apple Toast

Preparation Time: 15 minutes

Cooking Time: 0 minute

Servings: 1

Ingredients:

- 2 Tablespoons Tahini
- 2 Slices Whole Wheat Bread, Toasted
- 1 Teaspoon Honey, Raw
- 1 Apple, Small, Cored & Sliced Thin

Directions:

- Start by spreading the tahini over your toast, and then lay your apples over it. drizzle with honey before serving.

Per serving: Calories: 111; Sodium: 543mg; Carbohydrates: 16g; Fiber: 12g; Protein: 38g

- ## Scrambled Basil Eggs

Preparation Time: 5 minutes

Cooking Time: 10 minutes

Servings: 2

Ingredients:

- 4 Eggs, Large
- 2 Tablespoons Fresh Basil, Chopped Fine
- 2 Tablespoons Gruyere Cheese, Grated
- 1 Tablespoon Cream
- 1 Tablespoon Olive Oil
- 2 Cloves Garlic, Minced
- Sea Salt & Black Pepper to Taste

Directions:

- Get out a large bowl and beat your basil, cheese, cream and eggs together. Whisk until it's well combined. Get out a large skillet over medium-low heat, and heat your oil. Add in your garlic, cooking for a minute. It should turn golden.
- Pour the egg mixture into your skillet over the garlic, and then continue to scramble as they cook so they become soft and fluffy. Season it well and serve warm.

Per serving: Calories: 111; Sodium: 543mg; Carbohydrates: 16g; Fiber: 12g; Protein: 38g

• Greek Potatoes & Eggs

Preparation Time: 10 minutes

Cooking Time: 30 minutes

Servings: 2

Ingredients:

- 3 tomatoes, seeded & roughly chopped
- 2 tablespoons basil, fresh & chopped
- 1 clove garlic, minced
- 2 tablespoons + ½ cup olive oil, divided
- sea salt & black pepper to taste
- 3 russet potatoes, large
- 4 eggs, large
- 1 teaspoon oregano, fresh & chopped

Directions:

- Get the food processor and place your tomatoes in, pureeing them with the skin on.
- Add your garlic, two tablespoons of oil, salt, pepper and basil. Pulse until it's well combined. Place this mixture in a skillet, cooking while covered for twenty to twenty-five minutes over low heat. Your sauce should be thickened as well as bubbly.

- Dice your potatoes into cubes, and then place them in a skillet with a ½ a cup of olive oil in a skillet using medium-low heat.
- Fry your potatoes until crisp and browned. This should take five minutes, and then cover the skillet, reducing the heat to low. Steam them until your potatoes are done.
- Stir in the eggs into the tomato sauce, and cook using low heat for six minutes. Your eggs should be set.
- Remove the potatoes from your pan, and drain using paper towels. Place them in a bowl. Sprinkle in your salt, pepper and oregano, and then serve your eggs with potatoes. Drizzle your sauce over the mixture, and serve warm.

Per serving: Calories: 111; Sodium: 543mg; Carbohydrates: 16g; Fiber: 12g; Protein: 38g

• Avocado & Honey Smoothie

Preparation Time: 5 minutes

Cooking Time: 0 minute

Servings: 2

Ingredients:

- 1 1/2 cups soy milk
- 1 avocado, large
- 2 tablespoons honey, raw

Directions:

- Incorporate all ingredients together and blend until smooth, and serve immediately.

Per serving: Calories: 111; Sodium: 543mg; Carbohydrates: 16g; Fiber: 12g; Protein: 38g

• Vegetable Frittata

Preparation Time: 5 minutes

Cooking Time: 10 minutes

Servings: 2

Ingredients:

- 1/2 baby eggplant, peeled & diced
- 1 handful baby spinach leaves
- 1 tablespoon olive oil
- 3 eggs, large
- 1 teaspoon almond milk
- 1-ounce goat cheese, crumbled
- 1/4 small red pepper, chopped
- sea salt & black pepper to taste

Directions:

- Start by heating the broiler on your oven, and then beat the eggs together with almond milk. Make sure it's well combined, and then get out a nonstick, oven proof skillet. Place it over medium-high heat, and then add in your olive oil.
- Once your oil is heated, add in your eggs. Spread your spinach over this mixture in an even layer, and top with the rest of your vegetables.
- Reduce your heat to medium, and sprinkle with salt and pepper. Allow your vegetables and eggs to cook for five minutes. The bottom half of your eggs should be firm, and your vegetables should be tender. Top with goat cheese, and then broil on the middle rack for three to five minutes. Your eggs should be all the way done, and your cheese should be melted. Slice into wedges and serve warm.

Per serving: Calories: 111; Sodium: 543mg; Carbohydrates: 16g; Fiber: 12g; Protein: 38g

Mini Lettuce Wraps

Preparation Time: 15 minutes

Cooking Time: 0 minute

Servings: 4

Ingredients:

- 1 cucumber, diced

- 1 red onion, sliced

- 1-ounce feta cheese, low fat & crumbed

- 1 lemon, juiced

- 1 tomato, diced

- 1 tablespoon olive oil

- 12 small iceberg lettuce leaves

- sea salt & black pepper to taste

Directions:

- Combine your tomato, onion, feta, and cucumber together in a bowl. Mix your oil and juice, and season with salt and pepper.

- Fill each leaf with the vegetable mixture, and roll them tightly. Use a toothpick to keep them together to serve.

Per serving: Calories: 111; Sodium: 543mg; Carbohydrates: 16g; Fiber: 12g; Protein: 38g

• Curry Apple Couscous

Preparation Time: 20 minutes

Cooking Time: 5 minutes

Servings: 4

Ingredients:

- 2 teaspoons olive oil

- 2 leeks, white parts only, sliced

- 1 apple, diced

- 2 tablespoons curry powder

- 2 cups couscous, cooked & whole wheat

- 1/2 cup pecans, chopped

Directions:

- Heat your oil in a skillet using medium heat. Add the leeks, and cook until tender, which will take five minutes. Add in your apple, and cook until soft.

- Add in your curry powder and couscous, and stir well. Remove from heat, and mix in your nuts before serving immediately.

Per serving: Calories: 234; Sodium: 543mg; Carbohydrates: 16g; Fiber: 12g; Protein: 38g

Dessert

- ## Butter Pie

Preparation Time: 10 minutes

Cooking Time: 15 minutes

Servings: 2

Ingredients:

- 3 whole eggs
- 6 tbsp of all-purpose flour
- 1 ½ cup of milk
- Salt to taste
- 4 tbsp of butter
- 1 cup of skim sour cream
- 1 tbsp of ground red pepper

Directions:

- Preheat the oven to 300°. Line in some baking paper over a baking dish and then set it aside.

- Mix well three eggs, all-purpose flour, 2 table spoons of butter, milk, and salt. Spread the mixture on a baking dish and then bake it for about 15 minutes.

- When done, remove from the oven and cool for a while. Chop into bite-sized pieces and place on a serving plate. Pour 1 cup of sour cream.

- Melt the remaining 2 table spoons of butter over a medium temperature. Add 1 tablespoon of ground red pepper and stir-fry for several minutes. Drizzle some of this mixture over the pie and serve immediately.

Per serving: Calories: 211; Sodium: 543mg; Carbohydrates: 16g; Fiber: 12g; Protein: 38g

- ## Homemade Spinach Pie

Preparation Time: 20 minutes

Cooking Time: 30 minutes

Servings: 5

Ingredients:

- 1lb. fresh spinach
- 0.5 lb. fresh dandelion leaves
- ¼ cup of Feta cheese, crumbled
- ½ cup of sour cream
- ½ cup of blue cheese, chopped
- 2 eggs
- 2 tbsp of butter, melted
- Salt to taste
- 1 pack of pie crust
- Vegetable oil

Directions:

- Preheat the oven to 350 degrees. Use 1 table spoon of butter to grease the baking dish.
- Add the ingredients in a large bowl and then mix well. Grease the pie crust with some oil. Spread the spinach mixture over the pie crust and roll. Place in a baking dish and then bake for about 30-40 minutes
- Remove from the heat and serve warm.

Per serving: Calories: 111; Sodium: 543mg; Carbohydrates: 16g; Fiber: 12g; Protein: 38g

- ## Rhubarb Strawberry Crunch

Preparation Time: 20 minutes

Cooking Time: 60 minutes

Servings: 18

Ingredients:

- 3 tbsps. all-purpose flour

- 3 c. fresh strawberries, sliced
- 3 c. rhubarb, cubed
- 1 ½ c. flour
- 1 c. packed brown sugar
- 1 c. butter
- 1 c. oatmeal

Directions:

- Preheat the oven to 374°F
- In a medium bowl mix rhubarb, 3 tbsps. flour, white sugar, and strawberries. Set the mixture in a baking dish.
- In another bowl mix 1 ½ cups of flour, brown sugar, butter, and oats until a crumbly texture is obtained. You may use a blender.
- Combine mixtures and place on the baking pan
- Bake for 45 minutes or until crispy and light brown.

Per serving: Calories: 211; Sodium: 543mg; Carbohydrates: 16g; Fiber: 12g; Protein: 38g

• Banana Dessert with Chocolate Chips

Preparation Time: 20 minutes

Cooking Time: 30 minutes

Servings: 24

Ingredients:

- 2/3 c. white sugar
- ¾ c. butter
- 2/3 c. brown sugar
- 1 egg, beaten
- 1 tsp. vanilla extract
- 1 c. banana puree
- 1 ¾ c. flour

- 2 tsps. baking powder
- ½ tsp. salt
- 1 c. semi-sweet chocolate chips

Directions:

- Preheat oven at 350°F
- In a bowl, add the sugars and butter and beat until lightly colored
- Add the egg and vanilla.
- Add the banana puree and stir
- In another bowl mix baking powder, flour, and salt. Add this mixture to the butter mixture
- Stir in the chocolate chips
- Prepare a baking pan and place the dough onto it
- Bake for 20 minutes and let it cool for 5 minutes before slicing into equal squares

Per serving: Calories: 111; Sodium: 543mg; Carbohydrates: 16g; Fiber: 12g; Protein: 38g

• Mascarpone and Fig Crostini

Preparation Time: 10 minutes

Cooking Time: 10 minutes

Servings: 6-8

Ingredients:

- 1 long French baguette
- 4 tablespoons (½ stick) salted butter, melted
- 1 (8-ounce) tub mascarpone cheese
- 1 (12-ounce) jar fig jam or preserves

Directions:

- Preheat the oven to 350°F.
- Slice the bread into ¼-inch-thick slices.

- Lay out the sliced bread on a single baking sheet and brush each slice with the melted butter.
- Put the single baking sheet in the oven and toast the bread for 5 to 7 minutes, just until golden brown.
- Let the bread cool slightly. Spread it about a tea spoon or so of the mascarpone cheese on each piece of bread.
- Top with a teaspoon or so of the jam. Serve immediately.

Per serving: Calories: 411; Sodium: 543mg; Carbohydrates: 16g; Fiber: 12g; Protein: 38g

• Crunchy Sesame Cookies

Preparation Time: 10 minutes

Cooking Time: 15 minutes

Servings: 14-16

Ingredients:

- 1 cup sesame seeds, hulled
- 1 cup sugar
- 8 tablespoons (1 stick) salted butter, softened
- 2 large eggs
- 1¼ cups flour

Directions:

- Preheat the oven to 350°F. Toast the sesame seeds on a baking sheet for 3 minutes. Set aside and let cool.
- Using a mixer, cream together the sugar and butter.
- Put the eggs one at a time until well-blended.
- Add the flour and toasted sesame seeds and mix until well-blended.
- Drop spoonful of cookie dough onto a baking sheet and form them into round balls, about 1-inch in diameter, similar to a walnut.
- Put in the oven and bake for 5 to 7 minutes or until golden brown.
- Let the cookies cool and enjoy.

Per serving: Calories: 111; Sodium: 543mg; Carbohydrates: 16g; Fiber: 12g; Protein: 38g

• Almond Cookies

Preparation Time: 5 minutes

Cooking Time: 10 minutes

Servings: 4-6

Ingredients:

- ½ cup sugar
- 8 tablespoons (1 stick) room temperature salted butter
- 1 large egg
- 1½ cups all-purpose flour
- 1 cup ground almonds or almond flour

Directions:

- Preheat the oven to 375°F.
- Using a mixer, cream together the sugar and butter.
- Add the egg and mix until combined.
- Alternately add the flour and ground almonds, ½ cup at a time, while the mixer is on slow.
- Once everything is combined, line a baking sheet with parchment paper. Drop a tablespoon of dough on the baking sheet, keeping the cookies at least 2 inches apart.
- Put the single baking sheet in the oven and bake just until the cookies start to turn brown around the edges for about 5 to 7 minutes.

Per serving: Calories: 222; Sodium: 543mg; Carbohydrates: 16g; Fiber: 12g; Protein: 38g

• Baklava and Honey

Preparation Time: 40 minutes

Cooking Time: 1 hour

Servings: 6-8

Ingredients:

- 2 cups chopped walnuts or pecans
- 1 teaspoon cinnamon
- 1 cup of melted unsalted butter
- 1 (16-ounce) package phyllo dough, thawed
- 1 (12-ounce) jar honey

Directions:

- Preheat the oven to 350°F.
- In a bowl, combine the chopped nuts and cinnamon.
- Using a brush, butter the sides and bottom of a 9-by-13-inch inch baking dish.
- Take off the phyllo dough from the package and cut it to the size of the baking dish using a sharp knife.
- Put one sheet of phyllo dough on the bottom of the dish, brush with butter, and repeat until you have 8 layers.
- Sprinkle ⅓ cup of the nut mixture over the phyllo layers. Top with a sheet of phyllo dough, butter that sheet, and repeat until you have 4 sheets of buttered phyllo dough.
- Sprinkle ⅓ cup of the nut mixture for another layer of nuts. Repeat the layering of nuts and 4 sheets of buttered phyllo until all the nut mixture is gone. The last layer should be 8 buttered sheets of phyllo.
- Before you bake, cut the baklava into desired shapes; traditionally this is diamonds, triangles, or squares.
- Bake the baklava for about 1 hour just until the top layer is golden brown.
- While the baklava is baking, heat the honey in a pan just until it is warm and easy to pour.
- Once the baklava is done baking, directly pour the honey evenly over the baklava and let it absorb it, about 20 minutes. Serve warm or at room temperature.

Per serving: Calories: 111; Sodium: 543mg; Carbohydrates: 16g; Fiber: 12g; Protein: 38g

- ## Date and Nut Balls

Preparation Time: 10 minutes

Cooking Time: 10 minutes

Servings: 6-8

Ingredients:

- 1 cup walnuts or pistachios
- 1 cup unsweetened shredded coconut
- 14 medjool dates, pits removed
- 8 tablespoons (1 stick) butter, melted

Directions:

- Preheat the oven to 350°F.
- Put the nuts on a baking sheet. Toast the nuts for 5 minutes.
- Put the shredded coconut on a clean baking sheet; toast just until it turns golden brown, about 3 to 5 minutes (coconut burns fast so keep an eye on it). Once done, remove it from the oven and put it in a shallow bowl.
- Inside a food processor with a chopping blade, put the nuts until they have a medium chop. Put the chopped nuts into a medium bowl.
- Add the dates and melted butter to the food processor and blend until the dates become a thick paste. Pour the chopped nuts into the food processor with the dates and pulse just until the mixture is combined, about 5 to 7 pulses.
- Remove the mixture from the food processor and scrape it into a large bowl.
- To make the balls, spoon 1 to 2 tablespoons of the date mixture into the palm of your hand and roll around between your hands until you form a ball. Put the ball on a clean, lined baking sheet. Repeat this until all of the mixture is formed into balls.
- Roll each ball in the toasted coconut until the outside of the ball is coated, put the ball back on the baking sheet, and repeat.
- Put all the balls into the fridge for 20 minutes before serving so that they firm up. You can also store any leftovers inside the fridge in an airtight container.

Per serving: Calories: 233; Sodium: 543mg; Carbohydrates: 16g; Fiber: 12g; Protein: 38g

• Creamy Rice Pudding

Preparation Time: 5 minutes

Cooking Time: 45 minutes

Servings: 6

Ingredients:

- 1¼ cups long-grain rice
- 5 cups whole milk
- 1 cup sugar
- 1 tablespoon of rose water/orange blossom water
- 1 teaspoon cinnamon

Directions:

- Rinse the rice under cold water for 30 seconds.
- Add the rice, milk, and sugar in a large pot. Bring to a gentle boil while continually stirring.
- Lessen the heat to low and then let simmer for 40 to 45 minutes, stirring every 3 to 4 minutes so that the rice does not stick to the bottom of the pot.
- Add the rose water at the end and simmer for 5 minutes.
- Divide the pudding into 6 bowls. Sprinkle the top with cinnamon. Let it cool for over an hour before serving. Store in the fridge.

Per serving: Calories: 345; Sodium: 543mg; Carbohydrates: 16g; Fiber: 12g; Protein: 38g

• Ricotta-Lemon Cheesecake

Preparation Time: 5 minutes

Cooking Time: 1 hour

Servings: 8-10

Ingredients:

- 2 (8-ounce) packages full-fat cream cheese
- 1 (16-ounce) container full-fat ricotta cheese
- 1½ cups granulated sugar
- 1 tablespoon lemon zest
- 5 large eggs
- Nonstick cooking spray

Directions:

- Preheat the oven to 350°F.
- Blend together the cream cheese and ricotta cheese.
- Blend in the sugar and lemon zest.
- Blend in the eggs; drop in 1 egg at a time, blend for 10 seconds, and repeat.
- Put a 9-inch springform pan with a parchment paper and nonstick spray. Wrap the bottom of the pan with foil. Pour the cheesecake batter into the pan.
- To make a water bath, get a baking or roasting pan larger than the cheesecake pan. Fill the roasting pan about ⅓ of the way up with warm water. Put the cheesecake pan into the water bath. Put the whole thing in the oven and let the cheesecake bake for 1 hour.
- After baking is complete, remove the cheesecake pan from the water bath and remove the foil. Let the cheese cake cool for 1 hour on the countertop. Then put it in the fridge to cool for at least 3 hours before serving.

Per serving: Calories: 365; Sodium: 543mg; Carbohydrates: 16g; Fiber: 12g; Protein: 38g

• Crockpot Chocolate Cake

Preparation Time: 20 minutes

Cooking Time: 3 hours

Servings: 12

Ingredients:

- ¾ c. stevia sweetener
- 1 ½ c. almond flour

- ¼ tsp. baking powder
- ¼ c. protein powder, chocolate, or vanilla flavor
- 2/3 c. unsweetened cocoa powder
- ¼ tsp. salt
- ½ c. unsalted butter, melted
- 4 large eggs
- ¾ c. heavy cream
- 1 tsp. vanilla extract

Directions:

- Grease the ceramic insert of the Crockpot.
- In a bowl, mix the sweetener, almond flour, protein powder, cocoa powder, salt, and baking powder.
- Add the butter, eggs, cream, and vanilla extract.
- Pour the batter in the Crockpot and cook on low for 3 hours.
- Allow to cool before slicing.

serving: Calories: 233; Sodium: 543mg; Carbohydrates: 16g; Fiber: 12g; Protein: 38g

- **Lava Cake**

Preparation Time: 30 minutes

Cooking Time: 3 hours

Servings: 12

Ingredients:

- 1 ½ c. stevia sweetener, divided
- ½ c. almond flour
- 5 tbsps. unsweetened cocoa powder
- ½ tsp. salt
- 1 tsp. baking powder
- 3 whole eggs
- 3 egg yolks

- ½ c. butter, melted
- 1 tsp. vanilla extract
- 2 c. hot water
- 4 ounces sugar-free chocolate chips

Directions:

- Grease the inside of the Crockpot.
- In a bowl, mix the stevia sweetener, almond flour, cocoa powder, salt, and baking powder.
- In another bowl, mix the eggs, egg yolks, butter, and vanilla extract. Pour in the hot water.
- Pour the wet ingredients to the dry ingredients and fold to create a batter.
- Add the chocolate chips last
- Pour into the greased Crockpot and cook on low for 3 hours.
- Allow to cool before serving.

Per serving: Calories: 111; Sodium: 543mg; Carbohydrates: 16g; Fiber: 12g; Protein: 38g

• Lemon Crockpot Cake

Preparation Time: 15 minutes

Cooking Time: 3 hours

Servings: 8

Ingredients:

- ½ c. coconut flour
- 1 ½ c. almond flour
- 3 tbsps. stevia sweetener
- 2 tsps. baking powder
- ½ tsp. xanthan gum
- ½ c. whipping cream
- ½ c. butter, melted

- 1 tbsp. juice, freshly squeezed
- Zest from one large lemon
- 2 eggs

Directions:

- Grease the inside of the Crockpot with a butter or cooking spray.
- Mix together coconut flour, almond flour, stevia, baking powder, and xanthan gum in a bowl.
- In another bowl, combine the whipping cream, butter, lemon juice, lemon zest, and eggs. Mix until well combined.
- Pour the wet ingredients to the dry ingredients gradually and fold to create a smooth batter.
- Spread the batter in the Crockpot and cook on low for 3 hours

Per serving: Calories: 111; Sodium: 543mg; Carbohydrates: 16g; Fiber: 12g; Protein: 38g

- ## Lemon and Watermelon Granita

Preparation Time: 10 minutes + 3 hours to freeze

Cooking Time: None

Servings: 4

Ingredients:

- 4 cups watermelon cubes
- ¼ cup honey
- ¼ cup freshly squeezed lemon juice

Directions:

- In a blender, combine the watermelon, honey, and lemon juice. Purée all the ingredients, then pour into a 9-by-9-by-2-inch baking pan and place in the freezer.
- Every 30 to 60 minutes, run a fork across the frozen surface to fluff and create ice flakes. Freeze for about 3 hours total and serve.

Per serving: Calories: 256; Sodium: 543mg; Carbohydrates: 16g; Fiber: 12g; Protein: 38g

Vegetable

- ## Mushroom and Cheese Stuffed Tomatoes

Preparation Time: 15 minutes

Cooking Time: 20 minutes

Serving: 4

Size/ Portion: 1 piece

Ingredients:

- 4 large ripe tomatoes
- 1 tablespoon olive oil
- ½ pound (454 g) white or cremini mushrooms
- 1 tablespoon fresh basil, chopped
- ½ cup yellow onion, diced
- 1 tablespoon fresh oregano, chopped
- 2 garlic cloves, minced
- ½ teaspoon salt
- ¼ teaspoon freshly ground black pepper
- 1 cup part-skim Mozzarella cheese, shredded
- 1 tablespoon Parmesan cheese, grated

Direction:

- Set oven to 375°F (190°C).
- Chop a ½-inch slice off the top of each tomato. Scoop the pulp into a bowl and leave ½-inch tomato shells. Arrange the tomatoes on a baking sheet lined with aluminum foil.
- Heat the olive oil in a nonstick skillet over medium heat.
- Add the mushrooms, basil, onion, oregano, garlic, salt, and black pepper to the skillet and sauté for 5 minutes

- Pour the mixture to the bowl of tomato pulp, then add the Mozzarella cheese and stir to combine well.
- Spoon the mixture into each tomato shell, then top with a layer of Parmesan.
- Bake for 15 minutes
- Remove the stuffed tomatoes from the oven and serve warm.

Per serving: Calories: 233; Sodium: 543mg; Carbohydrates: 16g; Fiber: 12g; Protein: 38g

- ## Citrus Pistachios and Asparagus

Preparation Time: 10 minutes

Cooking Time: 10 minutes

Serving: 4

Size/ Portion:

Ingredients:

- Zest and juice of 2 clementine
- Zest and juice of 1 lemon
- 1 tablespoon red wine vinegar
- 3 tablespoons extra-virgin olive oil
- 1 teaspoon salt
- ¼ teaspoon black pepper
- ½ cup pistachios, shelled
- 1-pound fresh asparagus
- 1 tablespoon water

Direction:

- Combine the zest and juice of clementine and lemon, vinegar, 2 tablespoons of olive oil, ½ teaspoon of salt, and black pepper in a bowl. Stir to mix well. Set aside.
- Toast the pistachios in a nonstick skillet over medium-high heat for 2 minutes or until golden brown. Transfer the roasted pistachios to a clean work surface, then chop roughly. Mix the pistachios with the citrus mixture. Set aside.

- Heat the remaining olive oil in the nonstick skillet over medium-high heat.
- Add the asparagus to the skillet and sauté for 2 minutes, then season with remaining salt.
- Add the water to the skillet. Turn down the heat to low, and put the lid on. Simmer for 4 minutes until the asparagus is tender.
- Remove the asparagus from the skillet to a large dish. Pour the citrus and pistachios mixture over the asparagus. Toss to coat well before serving.

Per serving: Calories: 211; Sodium: 543mg; Carbohydrates: 16g; Fiber: 12g; Protein: 38g

• Tomato and Parsley Stuffed Eggplant

Preparation Time: 25 minutes

Cooking Time: 2 hours

Serving: 6

Size/ portion: ½ cup

Ingredients:

- ¼ cup extra-virgin olive oil
- 3 small eggplants, cut in half lengthwise
- 1 teaspoon sea salt
- ½ teaspoon freshly ground black pepper
- 1 large yellow onion, finely chopped
- 4 garlic cloves, minced
- 15 ounces diced tomatoes
- ¼ cup fresh flat-leaf parsley

Direction:

- Brush inserts of the slow cooker with 2 tablespoons of olive oil.
- Cut some slits on the cut side of each eggplant half, keep a ¼-inch space between each slit.
- Place the eggplant halves in the slow cooker, skin side down. Sprinkle with salt and black pepper.

- Cook remaining olive oil in a nonstick skillet over medium-high heat.
- Add the onion and garlic to the skillet and sauté for 3 minutes or until the onion is translucent.
- Add the parsley and tomatoes with the juice to the skillet, and sprinkle with salt and black pepper. Sauté for 5 more minutes or until they are tender.
- Divide and spoon the mixture in the skillet on the eggplant halves.
- Close and cook on HIGH for 2 hours.
- Transfer the eggplant to a plate, and allow to cool for a few minutes before serving.

Per serving: Calories: 111; Sodium: 543mg; Carbohydrates: 16g; Fiber: 12g; Protein: 38g

- ## Ratatouille

Preparation Time: 15 minutes

Cooking Time: 7 hours

Serving: 6

Size/ Portion: 2 ounces

Ingredient:

- 3 tablespoons extra-virgin olive oil
- 1 large eggplant
- 2 large onions
- 4 small zucchinis
- 2 green bell peppers
- 6 large tomatoes
- 2 tablespoons fresh flat-leaf parsley
- 1 teaspoon dried basil
- 2 garlic cloves, minced
- 2 teaspoons sea salt
- ¼ teaspoon black pepper

Direction

- Grease inserts of the slow cooker with 2 tablespoons olive oil.
- Arrange the vegetables slices, strips, and wedges alternately in the insert of the slow cooker.
- Spread the parsley on top of the vegetables, and season with basil, garlic, salt, and black pepper. Drizzle with the remaining olive oil.
- Cover on and cook on LOW for 7 hours until the vegetables are tender.
- Transfer the vegetables on a plate and serve warm.

Per serving: Calories: 111; Sodium: 543mg; Carbohydrates: 16g; Fiber: 12g; Protein: 38g

- ## Gemista

Preparation Time: 15 minutes

Cooking Time: 4 hours

Serving: 4

Size/ portion: 2 ounces

Ingredients:

- 2 tablespoons extra-virgin olive oil
- 4 large bell peppers, any color
- ½ cup uncooked couscous
- 1 teaspoon oregano
- 1 garlic clove, minced
- 1 cup crumbled feta cheese
- 1 (15-ounce) can cannellini beans
- 4 green onions

Direction:

- Brush inserts of the slow cooker with 2 tablespoons olive oil.
- Cut a ½-inch slice below the stem from the top of the bell pepper. Discard the stem only and chop the sliced top portion under the stem, and reserve in a bowl. Hollow the bell pepper with a spoon.

- Mix remaining ingredients, except for the green parts of the green onion and lemon wedges, to the bowl of chopped bell pepper top. Stir to mix well.
- Spoon the mixture in the hollowed bell pepper, and arrange the stuffed bell peppers in the slow cooker, then drizzle with more olive oil.
- Close and cook at HIGH for 4 hours or until the bell peppers are soft.
- Remove the bell peppers from the slow cooker and serve on a plate. Sprinkle with green parts of the green onions, and squeeze the lemon wedges on top before serving.

Per serving: Calories: 111; Sodium: 543mg; Carbohydrates: 16g; Fiber: 12g; Protein: 38g

- **Stuffed Cabbage Rolls**

Preparation Time: 15 minutes

Cooking Time: 2 hours

Serving: 4

Size/ Portion: 1 roll

Ingredients:

- 4 tablespoons olive oil
- 1 large head green cabbage
- 1 large yellow onion
- 3 ounces (85 g) feta cheese
- ½ cup dried currants
- 3 cups cooked pearl barley
- 2 tablespoons fresh flat-leaf parsley
- 2 tablespoons pine nuts, toasted
- ½ teaspoon sea salt
- ½ teaspoon black pepper
- 15 ounces (425 g) crushed tomatoes, with the juice
- ½ cup apple juice
- 1 tablespoon apple cider vinegar

Direction:

- Rub insert of the slow cooker with 2 tablespoons olive oil.
- Blanch the cabbage in a pot of water for 8 minutes. Remove it from the water, and allow to cool, then separate 16 leaves from the cabbage. Set aside.
- Drizzle the remaining olive oil in a nonstick skillet, and heat over medium heat.
- Sauté onion for 6 minutes. Transfer the onion to a bowl.
- Add the feta cheese, currants, barley, parsley, and pine nuts to the bowl of cooked onion, then sprinkle with ¼ teaspoon of salt and ¼ teaspoon of black pepper.
- Arrange the cabbage leaves on a clean work surface. Spoon 1/3 cup of the mixture on the center of each leaf, then fold the edge of the leaf over the mixture and roll it up. Place the cabbage rolls in the slow cooker, seam side down.
- Combine the remaining ingredients in a separate bowl, then pour the mixture over the cabbage rolls.
- Close and cook in HIGH for 2 hours.
- Remove the cabbage rolls from the slow cooker and serve warm.

Per serving: Calories: 111; Sodium: 543mg; Carbohydrates: 16g; Fiber: 12g; Protein: 38g

• Brussels Sprouts with Balsamic Glaze

Preparation Time: 15 minutes

Cooking Time: 2 hours

Serving: 6

Size/ Portion: 1 lb.

Balsamic glaze:

- 1 cup balsamic vinegar
- ¼ cup honey

Other:

- 2 tablespoons extra-virgin olive oil
- 2 pounds (907 g) Brussels sprouts
- 2 cups low-sodium vegetable soup

- 1 teaspoon sea salt
- Freshly ground black pepper, to taste
- ¼ cup Parmesan cheese, grated
- ¼ cup pine nuts, toasted

Direction:

- Brush inserts of the slow cooker with olive oil.
- Make the balsamic glaze: Combine the balsamic vinegar and honey in a saucepan. Stir to mix well. Over medium-high heat, bring to a boil. Turn down the heat to low, then simmer for 20 minutes or until the glaze reduces in half and has a thick consistency.
- Put the Brussels sprouts, vegetable soup, and ½ teaspoon of salt in the slow cooker, stir to combine.
- Cover and cook at HIGH for 2 hours.
- Transfer the Brussels sprouts to a plate, and sprinkle the remaining salt and black pepper to season. Drizzle the balsamic glaze over the Brussels sprouts, then serve with Parmesan and pine nuts.

Per serving: Calories: 344; Sodium: 543mg; Carbohydrates: 16g; Fiber: 12g; Protein: 38g

• Spinach Salad with Citrus Vinaigrette

Preparation Time: 10 minutes

Cooking Time: 0 minutes

Servings: 4

Size/ portion: 2 cups

Ingredients:

Citrus Vinaigrette:

- ¼ cup extra-virgin olive oil
- 3 tablespoons balsamic vinegar
- ½ teaspoon fresh lemon zest
- ½ teaspoon salt

SALAD:

- 1-pound (454 g) baby spinach
- 1 large ripe tomato
- 1 medium red onion

Direction:

- Make the citrus vinaigrette: Stir together the olive oil, balsamic vinegar, lemon zest, and salt in a bowl until mixed well.
- Make the salad: Place the baby spinach, tomato and onions in a separate salad bowl. Drizzle the citrus vinaigrette over the salad and gently toss until the vegetables are coated thoroughly.

Per serving: Calories: 111; Sodium: 543mg; Carbohydrates: 16g; Fiber: 12g; Protein: 38g

- ## Kale Salad with Pistachio and Parmesan

Preparation Time: 20 minutes

Cooking Time: 0 minutes

Serving: 6

Size/ Portion: 2 cups

Ingredients:

- 6 cups raw kale
- ¼ cup extra-virgin olive oil
- 2 tablespoons lemon juice
- ½ teaspoon smoked paprika
- 2 cups chopped arugula
- 1/3 cup unsalted pistachios
- 6 tablespoons Parmesan cheese

Direction:

- Put the kale, olive oil, lemon juice, and paprika in a large bowl. Using your hands to massage the sauce into the kale until coated completely. Allow the kale to marinate for about 10 minutes.

- When ready to serve, add the arugula and pistachios into the bowl of kale. Toss well and divide the salad into six salad bowls. Serve sprinkled with 1 tablespoon shredded Parmesan cheese.

Per serving: Calories: 111; Sodium: 543mg; Carbohydrates: 16g; Fiber: 12g; Protein: 38g

• Chinese Soy Eggplant

Preparation Time: 5 Minutes

Cooking Time: 10 Minutes

Servings: 2

Ingredients:

- Four tablespoons coconut oil
- Two eggplants, sliced into 3-inch in length
- Four cloves of garlic, minced
- One onion, chopped
- One teaspoon ginger, grated
- ¼ cup coconut aminos
- One teaspoon lemon juice, freshly squeezed

Directions:

- Heat oil in a pot.
- Pan-fry the eggplants for minutes on all sides.
- Add the garlic and onions until fragrant, around minutes.
- Stir in the ginger, coconut aminos, and lemon juice.
- Add a ½ cup of water and let it simmer. Cook until eggplant is tender.

Per serving: Calories: 111; Sodium: 543mg; Carbohydrates: 16g; Fiber: 12g; Protein: 38g

• Cauliflower Mash

Preparation Time: 5 Minutes

Cooking Time: 0 Minutes

Servings: 2

Ingredients:

- Crushed red pepper to taste
- 1 tsp fresh thyme
- 2 tsp chopped chives
- 2 tbsp. Nutritional yeast
- 2 tbsp. filtered water
- One garlic clove, peeled
- One lemon, juice extracted
- ¼ cup pine nuts
- 3 cups cauliflower, chopped

Directions:

- Mix all fixings in a blender or food processor. Pulse until smooth.
- Scoop into a bowl and add crushed red peppers.

Per serving: Calories: 111; Sodium: 543mg; Carbohydrates: 16g; Fiber: 12g; Protein: 38g

- ## Vegetarian Cabbage Rolls

Preparation Time: 5 Minutes

Cooking Time: 1 Hour and 30 Minutes

Servings: 2

Ingredients:

- One large head green cabbage
- 1 cup long-grain rice, rinsed
- Two medium zucchinis, finely diced
- 4 TB. minced garlic
- 2 tsp. salt
- 1 tsp. ground black pepper
- 4 cups plain tomato sauce

- 2 cups of water
- 1 tsp. dried mint

Directions:

- Cut around a core of cabbage with a knife, and remove the core. Put cabbage, with core side down, in a large, 3-quart pot. Cover cabbage with water, set over high heat, and cook for 30 minutes. Drain cabbage, set aside to cool, and separate leaves. (You need 24 leaves.)
- In a large bowl, combine long-grain rice, zucchini, one tablespoon garlic, one teaspoon salt, and 1/teaspoon black pepper.
- In a 2-quart pot, combine tomato sauce, water, remaining tablespoons garlic, mint, remaining one teaspoon salt, and 1/2 teaspoon black pepper.
- Lay each cabbage leaf flat on your work surface, spoon two tablespoons filling each leaf, and roll leaf. Layer rolls in a large pot, pour the sauce into the pot, cover, and cook over medium-low heat for 1 hour.
- Let rolls sit for 20 minutes before serving warm with Greek yogurt.

Per serving: Calories: 111; Sodium: 543mg; Carbohydrates: 16g; Fiber: 12g; Protein: 38g

• Vegan Sesame Tofu and Eggplants

Difficulty: Intermediate level

Preparation Time: 5 Minutes

Cooking Time: 15 Minutes

Servings: 4

Ingredients:

- Five tablespoons olive oil
- 1-pound firm tofu, sliced
- Three tablespoons rice vinegar
- Two teaspoons Swerve sweetener
- Two whole eggplants, sliced
- ¼ cup of soy sauce

- Salt and pepper to taste
- Four tablespoons toasted sesame oil
- ¼ cup sesame seeds
- 1 cup fresh cilantro, chopped

Directions:

- Heat the oil in a pan for 2 minutes.
- Pan-fry the tofu for 3 minutes on each side.
- Stir in the rice vinegar, sweetener, eggplants, and soy sauce—season with salt and pepper to taste.
- Close the lid, then cook for around 5 minutes on medium fire. Stir and continue cooking for another 5 minutes.
- Toss in the sesame oil, sesame seeds, and cilantro.
- Serve and enjoy.

Per serving: Calories: 111; Sodium: 543mg; Carbohydrates: 16g; Fiber: 12g; Protein: 38g

Seafood

- ## Pistachio-Crusted Whitefish

Preparation Time: 10 minutes

Cooking Time: 20 minutes

Servings: 2

Ingredients:

- ¼ cup shelled pistachios
- 1 tbsp. fresh parsley
- 1 tbsp. grated Parmesan cheese
- 1 tbsp. panko bread crumbs
- 2 tbsps. olive oil
- ¼ tsp. salt
- 10 oz. skinless whitefish (1 large piece or 2 smaller ones)

Directions:

- Preheat the oven to 350°F and set the rack to the middle position. Line a sheet pans with foil or parchment paper.
- Combine all of the ingredients except the fish in a mini food processor and pulse until the nuts are finely ground.
- Alternatively, you can mince the nuts with a chef's knife and combine the ingredients by hand in a small bowl.
- Place the fish on the sheet pan. Spread the nut mixture evenly over the fish and pat it down lightly.
- Bake the fish for 20 to 30 minutes, depending on the thickness, until it flakes easily with a fork.
- Keep in mind that a thicker cut of fish takes a bit longer to bake. You'll know it's done when it's opaque, flakes apart easily with a fork, or reaches an internal temperature of 145°F.

Per serving: Calories: 211; Sodium: 543mg; Carbohydrates: 16g; Fiber: 12g; Protein: 38g

• Grilled Fish on Lemons

Preparation Time: 10 minutes

Cooking Time: 10 minutes

Servings: 2

Ingredients:

- 4 (4-oz.) fish fillets, such as tilapia, salmon, catfish, cod, or your favorite fish
- Nonstick cooking spray
- 3 to 4 medium lemons
- 1 tbsp. extra-virgin olive oil
- ¼ tsp. freshly ground black pepper
- ¼ tsp. kosher or sea salt

Directions:

- Using paper towels pat the fillets dry and let stand at room temperature for 10 minutes.
- Meanwhile, coat the cold cooking grate of the grill with nonstick cooking spray and preheat the grill to 400°F, or medium-high heat. Or preheat a grill pan over medium-high heat on the stovetop.
- Cut 1 lemon in half and set half aside. Slice the remaining half of that lemon and the remaining lemons into ¼-inch-thick slices (You should have about 12 to 16 lemon slices).
- Into a small bowl, squeeze 1 tablespoon of juice out of the reserved lemon half.
- Add the oil to the bowl with the lemon juice and mix well.
- Brush both sides of the fish with the oil mixture and sprinkle evenly with pepper and salt.
- Carefully place the lemon slices on the grill (or the grill pan), arranging 3 to 4 slices together in the shape of a fish fillet and repeat with the remaining slices.

- Place the fish fillets directly on top of the lemon slices and grill with the lid closed (If you're grilling on the stovetop, cover with a large pot lid or aluminum foil).
- Turn the fish halfway through the cooking time only if the fillets are more than half an inch thick.
- The fish is done and ready to serve when it just begins to separate into flakes (chunks) when pressed gently with a fork.

Per serving: Calories: 111; Sodium: 543mg; Carbohydrates: 16g; Fiber: 12g; Protein: 38g

• Weeknight Sheet Pan Fish Dinner

Preparation Time: 10 minutes

Cooking Time: 10 minutes

Servings: 2

Ingredients:

- Nonstick cooking spray
- 2 tbsps. extra-virgin olive oil
- 1 tbsp. balsamic vinegar
- 4 (4-oz.) fish fillets, such as cod or tilapia (½ inch thick)
- 2½ cup green beans (about 12 oz.)
- 1-pint cherry or grape tomatoes (about 2 cups)

Directions:

- Preheat the oven to 400°F. Coat 2 large, rimmed baking sheets with nonstick cooking spray.
- In a small bowl, whisk together the oil and vinegar. Set aside. Place 2 pieces of fish on each baking sheet.
- In a large bowl, combine the beans and tomatoes. Pour in the oil and vinegar and toss gently to coat.
- Pour half of the green bean mixture over the fish on 1 baking sheet and the remaining half over the fish on the other.

- Turn the fish over and rub it in the oil mixture to coat. Spread the vegetables evenly on the baking sheets so hot air can circulate around them.
- Bake for 5 to 8 minutes, until the fish is just opaque and not translucent. The fish is done and ready to serve when it just begins to separate into flakes (chunks) when pressed gently with a fork.

Per serving: Calories: 111; Sodium: 543mg; Carbohydrates: 16g; Fiber: 12g; Protein: 38g

• Crispy Polenta Fish Sticks

Preparation Time: 15 minutes

Cooking Time: 10 minutes

Servings: 2

Ingredients:

- 2 large eggs, lightly beaten
- 1 tbsp. 2% milk
- 1 lb. skinned fish fillets (cod, tilapia, or other white fish) about ½ inch thick, sliced into 20 (1-inch-wide) strips
- ½ cup yellow cornmeal
- ½ cup whole-wheat panko bread crumbs or whole-wheat bread crumbs
- ¼ tsp. smoked paprika
- ¼ tsp. kosher or sea salt
- ¼ tsp. freshly ground black pepper
- Nonstick cooking spray

Directions:

- Place a large, rimmed baking sheet in the oven. Preheat the oven to 400°F with the pan inside. In a large bowl, mix the eggs and milk.
- Using a fork, add the fish strips to the egg mixture and stir gently to coat.
- Put the cornmeal, bread crumbs, smoked paprika, salt and pepper in a quart-size zip-top plastic bag.

- Using a fork or tongs, transfer the fish to the bag letting the excess egg wash drip off into the bowl before transferring. Seal the bag and shake gently to completely coat each fish stick.
- With oven mitts, carefully remove the hot baking sheet from the oven and spray it with nonstick cooking spray.
- Using a fork or tongs, remove the fish sticks from the bag and arrange them on the hot baking sheet, with space between them so the hot air can circulate and crisp them up.
- Bake for 5 to 8 minutes, until gentle pressure with a fork causes the fish to flake and serve.

Per serving: Calories: 111; Sodium: 543mg; Carbohydrates: 16g; Fiber: 12g; Protein: 38g

• Crispy Homemade Fish Sticks Recipe

Preparation Time: 10 minutes

Cooking Time: 15 minutes

Servings: 2

Ingredients:

- ½ cup flour
- 1 beaten egg
- 1 cup flour
- ½ cup parmesan cheese
- ½ cup bread crumbs.
- 1 lemon juice zest
- Parsley
- Salt
- 1 tsp. black pepper
- 1 tbsp. sweet paprika
- 1 tsp. oregano
- 1½ lb. salmon

- Extra virgin olive oil

Directions:

- Preheat your oven to about 450°F. Get a bowl, dry your salmon and season its 2 sides with the salt.
- Then chop into small sizes of 1½-inch length each. Get a bowl and mix black pepper with oregano.
- Add paprika to the mixture and blend it. Then spice the fish stick with the mixture you have just made. Get another dish and pour your flour.
- You will need a different bowl again to pour your egg wash into. Pick yet the fourth dish, mix your breadcrumb with your parmesan and add lemon zest to the mixture.
- Return to the fish sticks and dip each fish into flour such that both sides are coated with flour. As you dip each fish into flour, take it out and dip it into the egg wash and lastly. Dip it in the breadcrumb mixture.
- Do this for all fish sticks and arrange them on a baking sheet. Ensure you oil the baking sheet before arranging the stick thereon and drizzle the top of the fish sticks with extra virgin olive oil. zest, parsley and fresh lemon juice.

Per serving: Calories: 111; Sodium: 543mg; Carbohydrates: 16g; Fiber: 12g; Protein: 38g

- ## Sauced Shellfish in White Wine

Preparation Time: 10 minutes

Cooking Time: 10 minutes

Servings: 2

Ingredients:

- 2 lbs. fresh cuttlefish
- ½ cup olive oil
- 1 large onion, finely chopped
- 1 cup Robola white wine
- ¼ cup lukewarm water

- 1 bay leaf
- ½ bunch parsley, chopped
- 4 tomatoes, grated
- Salt and pepper

Directions:

- Take out the hard centerpiece of cartilage (cuttlebone), the bag of ink and the intestines from the cuttlefish.
- Wash the cleaned cuttlefish with running water. Slice it into small pieces and drain the excess water.
- Heat the oil in a saucepan placed over medium-high heat and sauté the onion for 3 minutes until tender.
- Add the sliced cuttlefish and pour in the white wine. Cook for 5 minutes until it simmers.
- Pour in the water and add the tomatoes, bay leaf, parsley, tomatoes, salt and pepper. Simmer the mixture over low heat until the cuttlefish slices are tender and left with their thick sauce. Serve them warm with rice.
- Be careful not to overcook the cuttlefish as its texture becomes very hard. A safe rule of thumb is grilling the cuttlefish over a ragingly hot fire for 3 minutes before using it in any recipe.

Per serving: Calories: 111; Sodium: 543mg; Carbohydrates: 16g; Fiber: 12g; Protein: 38g

- ## Pistachio Sole Fish

Preparation Time: 5 minutes

Cooking Time: 10 minutes

Servings: 2

Ingredients:

- 4 (5 oz.) boneless sole fillets
- ½ cup pistachios, finely chopped
- 1 lemon juice

- 1 tsp. extra virgin olive oil

Directions:

- Preheat your oven to 350°F.
- Wrap a baking sheet using parchment paper and keep it on the side.
- Pat fish dry with kitchen towels and lightly season with salt and pepper.
- Take a small bowl and stir in the pistachios.
- Place sole fillets on the prepped sheet and press 2 tablespoons of pistachio mixture on top of each fillet.
- Rub the fish with lemon juice and olive oil.
- Bake for 10 minutes until the top is golden and fish flakes with a fork.

Per serving: Calories: 101; Sodium: 543mg; Carbohydrates: 16g; Fiber: 12g; Protein: 38g

• Roasted Shrimp-Gnocchi Bake

Preparation Time: 10 minutes

Cooking Time: 20 minutes

Servings: 2

Ingredients:

- 1 cup chopped fresh tomato
- 2 tbsps. extra-virgin olive oil
- 2 garlic cloves, minced
- ½ tsp. freshly ground black pepper
- ¼ tsp. crushed red pepper
- 1 (12-oz.) jar roasted red peppers
- 1 lb. fresh raw shrimp, shells and tails removed
- 1 lb. frozen gnocchi (not thawed)
- ½ cup cubed feta cheese
- 1/3 cup fresh torn basil leaves

Directions:

- Preheat the oven to 425°F. In a baking dish, mix the tomatoes, oil, garlic, black pepper and crushed red pepper. Roast in the oven for 10 minutes.
- Stir in the roasted peppers and shrimp. Roast for 10 more minutes, until the shrimp turns pink and white.
- While the shrimp cooks, cook the gnocchi on the stovetop according to the package directions.
- Drain in a colander and keep warm. Remove the dish from the oven. Mix in the cooked gnocchi, feta and basil, and serve.

Per serving: Calories: 111; Sodium: 543mg; Carbohydrates: 16g; Fiber: 12g; Protein: 38g

• Slow Cooker Salmon in Foil

Preparation Time: 5 minutes

Cooking Time: 2 hours

Servings: 2

Ingredients:

- 2 (6-oz./170-g) salmon fillets
- 1 tbsp. olive oil
- 2 garlic cloves, minced
- ½ tbsp. lime juice
- 1 tsp. finely chopped fresh parsley
- ¼ tsp. black pepper

Direction

- Spread a length of foil onto a work surface and place the salmon fillets in the middle.
- Blend olive oil, garlic, lime juice, parsley and black pepper. Brush the mixture over the fillets. Fold the foil over and crimp the sides to make a packet.
- Place the packet into the slow cooker. Cover and cook on High for 2 hours
- Serve it hot.

Per serving: Calories: 101; Sodium: 543mg; Carbohydrates: 16g; Fiber: 12g; Protein: 38g

• Garlic-Butter Parmesan Salmon and Asparagus

Preparation Time: 10 minutes

Cooking Time: 15 minutes

Servings: 2

Ingredients:

- 2 (6-oz./170-g) salmon fillets, skin on and patted dry
- Pink Himalayan salt
- Freshly ground black pepper, to taste
- 1 lb. (454g) fresh asparagus, ends snapped off
- 3 tbsps. almond butter
- 2 garlic cloves, minced
- ¼ cup grated Parmesan cheese

Direction:

- Prep oven to 400 °F (205 °C). Line a baking sheet with aluminum foil.
- Season both sides of the salmon fillets.
- Situate the salmon in the middle of the baking sheet and arrange the asparagus around the salmon.
- Heat the almond butter in a small saucepan over medium heat.
- Cook the minced garlic
- Drizzle the garlic-butter sauce over the salmon and asparagus and scatter the Parmesan cheese on top.
- Bake in the preheated oven for about 12 minutes. You can switch the oven to broil at the end of cooking time for about 3 minutes to get a nice char on the asparagus.
- Let cool for 5 minutes before serving.

Per serving: Calories: 233; Sodium: 543mg; Carbohydrates: 16g; Fiber: 12g; Protein: 38g

- # Lemon Rosemary Roasted Branzino

Preparation Time: 15 minutes

Cooking Time: 30 minutes

Servings: 2

Ingredients:

- 4 tbsps. extra-virgin olive oil, divided
- 2 (8-oz.) Branzino fillets
- 1 garlic clove, minced
- 1 bunch scallions
- 10 to 12 small cherry tomatoes, halved
- 1 large carrot, cut into ¼-inch rounds
- ½ cup dry white wine
- 2 tbsps. paprika
- 2 tsps. kosher salt
- ½ tbsp. ground chili pepper
- 2 rosemary sprigs or 1 tbsp. dried rosemary
- 1 small lemon, thinly sliced
- ½ cup sliced pitted Kalamata olives

Direction:

- Heat a large ovenproof skillet over high heat until hot, about 2 minutes. Add 1 tbsp. of olive oil and heat it.
- Add the Branzino fillets, skin-side up, and sear for 2 minutes. Flip the fillets and cook. Set them aside.
- Swirl 2 tbsps. of olive oil around the skillet to coat evenly.
- Add the garlic, scallions, tomatoes, and carrot, and sauté for 5 minutes.
- Add the wine, stirring until all the ingredients are well combined. Carefully place the fish over the sauce.
- Preheat the oven to 450 °F (235 °C).

- Brush the fillets with the remaining 1 tablespoon of olive oil and season with paprika, salt and chili pepper. Top each fillet with a rosemary sprig and lemon slices. Scatter the olives over the fish and around the skillet.
- Roast for about 10 minutes until the lemon slices are browned. Serve it hot.

Per serving: Calories: 111; Sodium: 543mg; Carbohydrates: 16g; Fiber: 12g; Protein: 38g

• Grilled Lemon Pesto Salmon

Preparation Time: 5 minutes

Cooking Time: 10 minutes

Servings: 2

Ingredients:

- 10 oz. (283g) salmon fillet
- 2 tbsps. prepared pesto sauce
- 1 large fresh lemon, sliced
- Cooking spray

Direction:

- Preheat the grill to medium-high heat. Spray the grill grates with cooking spray.
- Season the salmon well. Spread the pesto sauce on top.
- Make a bed of fresh lemon slices about the same size as the salmon fillet on the hot grill and place the salmon on top of the lemon slices. Put any additional lemon slices on top of the salmon.
- Grill the salmon for 10 minutes.
- Serve it hot.

Per serving: Calories: 111; Sodium: 543mg; Carbohydrates: 16g; Fiber: 12g; Protein: 38g

• Steamed Trout with Lemon Herb Crust

Preparation Time: 10 minutes

Cooking Time: 15 minutes

Servings: 2

Ingredients:

- 3 tbsps. olive oil
- 3 garlic cloves, chopped
- 2 tbsps. fresh lemon juice
- 1 tbsp. chopped fresh mint
- 1 tbsp. chopped fresh parsley
- ¼ tsp. dried ground thyme
- 1 tsp. sea salt
- 1 lb. (454g) fresh trout (2 pieces)
- 2 cups fish stock

Direction:

- Blend olive oil, garlic, lemon juice, mint, parsley, thyme and salt. Brush the marinade onto the fish.
- Insert a trivet in the Instant Pot. Fill in the fish stock and place the fish on the trivet.
- Secure the lid. Select the Steam mode and set the cooking time for 15 minutes at High Pressure.
- Once cooking is complete, do a quick pressure release. Carefully open the lid. Serve warm.

Per serving: Calories: 211; Sodium: 543mg; Carbohydrates: 16g; Fiber: 12g; Protein: 38g

• Roasted Trout Stuffed with Veggies

Preparation Time: 10 minutes

Cooking Time: 25 minutes

Servings: 2

Ingredient:

- 2 (8-oz.) whole trout fillets
- 1 tbsp. extra-virgin olive oil

- ¼ tsp. salt
- 1/8 tsp. black pepper
- 1 small onion, thinly sliced
- ½ red bell pepper
- 1 Poblano pepper
- 2 or 3 shiitake mushrooms, sliced
- 1 lemon, sliced

Direction:

- Set the oven to 425 ºF (220 ºC). Coat a baking sheet with nonstick cooking spray.
- Rub both trout fillets, inside and out, with the olive oil. Season with salt and pepper.
- Mix together the onion, bell pepper, Poblano pepper and mushrooms in a large bowl. Stuff half of this mix into the cavity of each fillet. Top the mixture with 2 or 3 lemon slices inside each fillet.
- Place the fish on the prepared baking sheet side by side. Roast in the preheated oven for 25 minutes
- Then, pull out from the oven and serve on a plate.

Per serving: Calories: 111; Sodium: 543mg; Carbohydrates: 16g; Fiber: 12g; Protein: 38g

Poultry

- ## Chicken with Caper Sauce

Preparation Time: 20 minutes

Cooking Time: 18 minutes

Servings: 5

Ingredients:

- For Chicken:
- 2 eggs
- Salt and ground black pepper, as required
- 1 cup dry breadcrumbs
- 2 tablespoons olive oil
- 1½ pounds skinless, boneless chicken breast halves, pounded into ¾inch thickness and cut into pieces
- For Capers Sauce:
- 3 tablespoons capers
- ½ cup dry white wine
- 3 tablespoons fresh lemon juice
- Salt and ground black pepper, as required
- 2 tablespoons fresh parsley, chopped

Directions:

- For chicken: in a shallow dish, add the eggs, salt and black pepper and beat until well combined. In another shallow dish, place breadcrumbs. Soak the chicken pieces in egg mixture then coat with the breadcrumbs evenly. Shake off the excess breadcrumbs.
- Cook the oil over medium heat and cook the chicken pieces for about 5-7 minutes per side or until desired doneness. With a slotted spoon, situate the chicken pieces onto a paper towel lined plate. With a piece of the foil, cover the chicken pieces to keep them warm.

- In the same skillet, incorporate all the sauce ingredients except parsley and cook for about 2-3 minutes, stirring continuously. Mix in the parsley and remove from heat. Serve the chicken pieces with the topping of capers sauce.

Per serving: Calories: 111; Sodium: 543mg; Carbohydrates: 16g; Fiber: 12g; Protein: 38g

• Turkey Burgers with Mango Salsa

Preparation Time: 15 minutes

Cooking Time: 10 minutes

Servings: 6

Ingredients:

- 1½ pounds ground turkey breast
- 1 teaspoon sea salt, divided
- ¼ teaspoon freshly ground black pepper
- 2 tablespoons extra-virgin olive oil
- 2 mangos, peeled, pitted, and cubed
- ½ red onion, finely chopped
- Juice of 1 lime
- 1 garlic clove, minced
- ½ jalapeño pepper, seeded and finely minced
- 2 tablespoons chopped fresh cilantro leaves

Directions:

- Form the turkey breast into 4 patties and season with ½ teaspoon of sea salt and the pepper. Cook the olive oil in a nonstick skillet until it shimmers. Add the turkey patties and cook for about 5 minutes per side until browned. While the patties cook, mix together the mango, red onion, lime juice, garlic, jalapeño, cilantro, and remaining ½ teaspoon of sea salt in a small bowl. Spoon the salsa over the turkey patties and serve.

Per serving: Calories: 233; Sodium: 543mg; Carbohydrates: 16g; Fiber: 12g; Protein: 38g

• One-Pan Tuscan Chicken

Preparation Time: 10 minutes

Cooking Time: 25 minutes

Servings: 6

Ingredients:

- ¼ cup extra-virgin olive oil, divided
- 1-pound boneless, skinless chicken breasts, cut into ¾-inch pieces
- 1 onion, chopped
- 1 red bell pepper, chopped
- 3 garlic cloves, minced
- ½ cup dry white wine
- 1 (14-ounce) can crushed tomatoes, undrained
- 1 (14-ounce) can chopped tomatoes, drained
- 1 (14-ounce) can white beans, drained
- 1 tablespoon dried Italian seasoning
- ½ teaspoon sea salt
- 1/8 teaspoon freshly ground black pepper
- 1/8 teaspoon red pepper flakes
- ¼ cup chopped fresh basil leaves

Directions:

- Cook 2 tablespoons of olive oil until it shimmers. Mix in the chicken and cook until browned. Remove the chicken from the skillet and set aside on a platter, tented with aluminum foil to keep warm.

- Situate the skillet back to the heat and heat up the remaining olive oil. Add the onion and red bell pepper. Cook and stir rarely, until the vegetables are soft. Put the garlic and cook for 30 seconds, stirring constantly.

- Stir in the wine, and use the side of the spoon to scoop out any browned bits from the bottom of the pan. Cook for 1 minute, stirring.

- Mix in the crushed and chopped tomatoes, white beans, Italian seasoning, sea salt, pepper, and red pepper flakes. Allow to simmer. Cook for 5 minutes, stirring occasionally.
- Put the chicken back and any juices that have collected to the skillet. Cook until the chicken is cook through. Take out from the heat and stir in the basil before serving.

Per serving: Calories: 111; Sodium: 543mg; Carbohydrates: 16g; Fiber: 12g; Protein: 38g

• Chicken Kapama

Preparation Time: 10 minutes

Cooking Time: 2 hours

Servings: 4

Ingredients:

- 1 (32-ounce) can chopped tomatoes, drained
- ¼ cup dry white wine
- 2 tablespoons tomato paste
- 3 tablespoons extra-virgin olive oil
- ¼ teaspoon red pepper flakes
- 1 teaspoon ground allspice
- ½ teaspoon dried oregano
- 2 whole cloves
- 1 cinnamon stick
- ½ teaspoon sea salt
- 1/8 teaspoon freshly ground black pepper
- 4 boneless, skinless chicken breast halves

Directions:

- Mix the tomatoes, wine, tomato paste, olive oil, red pepper flakes, allspice, oregano, cloves, cinnamon stick, sea salt, and pepper in large pot. Bring to a simmer, stirring occasionally. Allow to simmer for 30 minutes, stirring occasionally. Remove and discard the whole cloves and cinnamon stick from the sauce and let the sauce cool.

- Preheat the oven to 350°F. Situate the chicken in a 9-by-13-inch baking dish. Pour the sauce over the chicken and cover the pan with aluminum foil. Continue baking until it reaches 165°F internal temperature.

Per serving: Calories: 111; Sodium: 543mg; Carbohydrates: 16g; Fiber: 12g; Protein: 38g

• Rosemary Baked Chicken Drumsticks

Preparation Time: 5 minutes

Cooking Time: 1 hour

Servings: 6

Ingredients:

- 2 tablespoons chopped fresh rosemary leaves
- 1 teaspoon garlic powder
- ½ teaspoon sea salt
- 1/8 teaspoon freshly ground black pepper
- Zest of 1 lemon
- 12 chicken drumsticks

Directions:

- Preheat the oven to 350°F. Mix the rosemary, garlic powder, sea salt, pepper, and lemon zest.
- Situate the drumsticks in a 9-by-13-inch baking dish and sprinkle with the rosemary mixture. Bake until the chicken reaches an internal temperature of 165°F.

Per serving: Calories: 222; Sodium: 543mg; Carbohydrates: 16g; Fiber: 12g; Protein: 38g

• Chicken with Onions, Potatoes, Figs, and Carrots

Preparation Time: 5 minutes

Cooking Time: 45 minutes

Servings: 4

Ingredients:

- 2 cups fingerling potatoes, halved
- 4 fresh figs, quartered
- 2 carrots, julienned
- 2 tablespoons extra-virgin olive oil
- 1 teaspoon sea salt, divided
- ¼ teaspoon freshly ground black pepper
- 4 chicken leg-thigh quarters
- 2 tablespoons chopped fresh parsley leaves

Directions:

- Preheat the oven to 425°F. In a small bowl, toss the potatoes, figs, and carrots with the olive oil, ½ teaspoon of sea salt, and the pepper. Spread in a 9-by-13-inch baking dish.
- Season the chicken with the rest of t sea salt. Place it on top of the vegetables. Bake until the vegetables are soft and the chicken reaches an internal temperature of 165°F. Sprinkle with the parsley and serve.

Per serving: Calories: 344; Sodium: 543mg; Carbohydrates: 16g; Fiber: 12g; Protein: 38g

- ## Moussaka

Preparation Time: 10 minutes

Cooking Time: 45 minutes

Servings: 8

Ingredients:

- 5 tablespoons extra-virgin olive oil, divided
- 1 eggplant, sliced (unpeeled)
- 1 onion, chopped
- 1 green bell pepper, seeded and chopped

- 1-pound ground turkey
- 3 garlic cloves, minced
- 2 tablespoons tomato paste
- 1 (14-ounce) can chopped tomatoes, drained
- 1 tablespoon Italian seasoning
- 2 teaspoons Worcestershire sauce
- 1 teaspoon dried oregano
- ½ teaspoon ground cinnamon
- 1 cup unsweetened nonfat plain Greek yogurt
- 1 egg, beaten
- ¼ teaspoon freshly ground black pepper
- ¼ teaspoon ground nutmeg
- ¼ cup grated Parmesan cheese
- 2 tablespoons chopped fresh parsley leaves

Directions:

- Preheat the oven to 400°F. Cook 3 tablespoons of olive oil until it shimmers. Add the eggplant slices and brown for 3 to 4 minutes per side. Transfer to paper towels to drain.

- Return the skillet back to the heat and pour the remaining 2 tablespoons of olive oil. Add the onion and green bell pepper. Continue cooking until the vegetables are soft. Remove from the pan and set aside.

- Pull out the skillet to the heat and stir in the turkey. Cook for about 5 minutes, crumbling with a spoon, until browned. Stir in the garlic and cook for 30 seconds, stirring constantly.

- Stir in the tomato paste, tomatoes, Italian seasoning, Worcestershire sauce, oregano, and cinnamon. Place the onion and bell pepper back to the pan. Cook for 5 minutes, stirring. Combine the yogurt, egg, pepper, nutmeg, and cheese.

- Arrange half of the meat mixture in a 9-by-13-inch baking dish. Layer with half the eggplant. Add the remaining meat mixture and the remaining eggplant.

Spread with the yogurt mixture. Bake until golden brown. Garnish with the parsley and serve.

Per serving: Calories: 211; Sodium: 543mg; Carbohydrates: 16g; Fiber: 12g; Protein: 38g

• Chicken in Tomato-Balsamic Pan Sauce

Preparation Time: 10 minutes

Cooking Time: 20 minutes

Servings: 4

Ingredients

- 2 (8 oz. or 226.7 g each) boneless chicken breasts, skinless
- ½ tsp. salt
- ½ tsp. ground pepper
- 3 tbsps. extra-virgin olive oil
- ½ c. halved cherry tomatoes
- 2 tbsps. sliced shallot
- ¼ c. balsamic vinegar
- 1 tbsp. minced garlic
- 1 tbsp. toasted fennel seeds, crushed
- 1 tbsp. butter

Directions;

- Slice the chicken breasts into 4 pieces and beat them with a mallet till it reaches a thickness of a ¼ inch. Use ¼ teaspoons of pepper and salt to coat the chicken. Heat two tablespoons of oil in a skillet and keep the heat to a medium. Cook the chicken breasts on both sides for three minutes. Place it to a serving plate and cover it with foil to keep it warm.
- Add one tablespoon oil, shallot, and tomatoes in a pan and cook till it softens. Add vinegar and boil the mix till the vinegar gets reduced by half. Put fennel seeds, garlic, salt, and pepper and cook for about four minutes. Pull it out from the heat and stir it with butter. Pour this sauce over chicken and serve.

Per serving: Calories: 211; Sodium: 543mg; Carbohydrates: 16g; Fiber: 12g; Protein: 38g

• Seasoned Buttered Chicken

Preparation Time: 10 minutes

Cooking Time: 20 minutes

Servings: 4

Ingredients

- ½ c. Heavy Whipping Cream
- 1 tbsp. Salt
- ½ c. Bone Broth
- 1 tbsp. Pepper
- 4 tbsps. Butter
- 4 Chicken Breast Halves

Directions:

- Place cooking pan on your oven over medium heat and add in one tablespoon of butter. Once the butter is warm and melted, place the chicken in and cook for five minutes on either side. At the end of this time, the chicken should be cooked through and golden; if it is, go ahead and place it on a plate.

- Next, you are going to add the bone broth into the warm pan. Add heavy whipping cream, salt, and pepper. Then, leave the pan alone until your sauce begins to simmer. Allow this process to happen for five minutes to let the sauce thicken up.

- Finally, you are going to add the rest of your butter and the chicken back into the pan. Be sure to use a spoon to place the sauce over your chicken and smother it completely. Serve

Per serving: Calories: 212; Sodium: 543mg; Carbohydrates: 16g; Fiber: 12g; Protein: 38g

- ## Double Cheesy Bacon Chicken

Preparation Time: 10 minutes

Cooking Time: 30 minutes

Servings: 4

Ingredients

- 4 oz. or 113 g. Cream Cheese
- 1 c. Cheddar Cheese
- 8 strips Bacon
- Sea salt
- Pepper
- 2 Garlic cloves, finely chopped
- Chicken Breast
- 1 tbsp. Bacon Grease or Butter

Directions:

- Ready the oven to 400 F/204 C Slice the chicken breasts in half to make them thin
- Season with salt, pepper, and garlic Grease a baking pan with butter and place chicken breasts into it. Add the cream cheese and cheddar cheese on top of the breasts
- Add bacon slices as well Place the pan to the oven for 30 minutes Serve hot

Per serving: Calories: 333; Sodium: 543mg; Carbohydrates: 16g; Fiber: 12g; Protein: 38g

- ## Chili Oregano Baked Cheese

Preparation Time: 10 minutes

Cooking Time: 25 minutes

Servings: 4

Ingredients

- 8 oz. or 226.7g feta cheese

- 4 oz. or 113g mozzarella, crumbled
- 1 sliced chili pepper
- 1 tsp. dried oregano
- 2 tbsps. olive oil

Directions:

- Place the feta cheese in a small deep-dish baking pan. Top with the mozzarella then season with pepper slices and oregano. cover your pan with lid. Bake in the preheated oven at 350 F/176 C for 20 minutes. Serve the cheese and enjoy it.

Per serving: Calories: 111; Sodium: 543mg; Carbohydrates: 16g; Fiber: 12g; Protein: 38g

• Crispy Italian Chicken

Preparation Time: 10 minutes

Cooking Time: 30 minutes

Servings: 4

Ingredients

- 4 chicken legs
- 1 tsp. dried basil
- 1 tsp. dried oregano
- Salt and pepper
- 3 tbsps. olive oil
- 1 tbsp. balsamic vinegar

Directions:

- Season the chicken well with basil, and oregano. Using a skillet, add oil and heat. Add the chicken in the hot oil. Let each side cook for 5 minutes until golden then cover the skillet with a lid.
- Adjust your heat to medium and cook for 10 minutes on one side then flip the chicken repeatedly, cooking for another 10 minutes until crispy. Serve the chicken and enjoy.

Per serving: Calories: 211; Sodium: 543mg; Carbohydrates: 16g; Fiber: 12g; Protein: 38g

- ## Sea Bass in a Pocket

Preparation Time: 10 minutes

Cooking Time: 25 minutes

Servings: 4

Ingredients

- 4 sea bass fillets
- 4 sliced garlic cloves
- 1 sliced celery stalk
- 1 sliced zucchini
- 1 c. halved cherry tomatoes halved
- 1 shallot, sliced
- 1 tsp. dried oregano
- Salt and pepper

Directions:

- Mix the garlic, celery, zucchini, tomatoes, shallot, and oregano in a bowl. Add salt and pepper to taste. Take 4 sheets of baking paper and arrange them on your working surface. Spoon the vegetable mixture in the center of each sheet.
- Top with a fish fillet then wrap the paper well so it resembles a pocket. Place the wrapped fish in a baking tray and cook in the preheated oven at 350 F/176 C for 15 minutes. Serve the fish warm and fresh.

Per serving: Calories: 214; Sodium: 543mg; Carbohydrates: 16g; Fiber: 12g; Protein: 38g

- ## Creamy Smoked Salmon Pasta

Preparation Time: 5 minutes

Cooking Time: 35 minutes

Servings: 4

Ingredients

- 2 tbsps. olive oil
- 2 chopped garlic cloves
- 1 shallot, chopped
- 4 oz. or 113 g chopped salmon, smoked
- 1 c. green peas
- 1 c. heavy cream
- Salt and pepper
- 1 pinch chili flakes
- 8 oz. or 230 g penne pasta
- 6 c. water

Directions:

- Place skillet on medium-high heat and add oil. Add the garlic and shallot. Cook for 5 minutes or until softened. Add peas, salt, pepper, and chili flakes. Cook for 10 minutes
- Add the salmon, and continue cooking for 5-7 minutes more. Add heavy cream, reduce heat and cook for an extra 5 minutes.
- In the meantime, place a pan with water and salt to your taste on high heat as soon as it boils, add penne pasta and cook for 8-10 minutes or until softened Drain the pasta, add to the salmon sauce and serve

Per serving: Calories: 111; Sodium: 543mg; Carbohydrates: 16g; Fiber: 12g; Protein: 38g

• Slow Cooker Greek Chicken

Preparation Time 20 minutes

Cooking Time: 3 hours

Servings: 4

Ingredients

- 1 tablespoon extra-virgin olive oil
- 2 pounds boneless, chicken breasts

- ½ tsp kosher salt
- ¼ tsp black pepper
- 1 (12-ounce) jar roasted red peppers
- 1 cup Kalamata olives
- 1 medium red onion, cut into chunks
- 3 tablespoons red wine vinegar
- 1 tablespoon minced garlic
- 1 teaspoon honey
- 1 teaspoon dried oregano
- 1 teaspoon dried thyme
- ½ cup feta cheese (optional, for serving)
- Chopped fresh herbs: any mix of basil, parsley, or thyme (optional, for serving)

Directions

- Brush slow cooker with nonstick cooking spray or olive oil. Cook the olive oil in a large skillet. Season both side of the chicken breasts. Once the oil is hot, add the chicken breasts and sear on both sides (about 3 minutes).
- Once cooked, transfer it to the slow cooker. Add the red peppers, olives, and red onion to the chicken breasts. Try to place the vegetables around the chicken and not directly on top.
- In a small bowl, mix together the vinegar, garlic, honey, oregano, and thyme. Once combined, pour it over the chicken. Cook the chicken on low for 3 hours or until no longer pink in the middle. Serve with crumbled feta cheese and fresh herbs.

Per serving: Calories: 111; Sodium: 543mg; Carbohydrates: 16g; Fiber: 12g; Protein: 38g

• Chicken Gyros

Preparation Time 10 minutes

Cooking Time: 4 hours

Servings: 4

Ingredients

- 2 lbs. boneless chicken breasts or chicken tenders
- Juice of one lemon
- 3 cloves garlic
- 2 teaspoons red wine vinegar
- 2–3 tablespoons olive oil
- ½ cup Greek yogurt
- 2 teaspoons dried oregano
- 2–4 teaspoons Greek seasoning
- ½ small red onion, chopped
- 2 tablespoons dill weed
- Tzatziki Sauce
- 1 cup plain Greek yogurt
- 1 tablespoon dill weed
- 1 small English cucumber, chopped
- Pinch of salt and pepper
- 1 teaspoon onion powder
- Toppings: tomatoes, chopped cucumbers, chopped red onion, diced feta cheese, crumbled pita bread

Directions

- Slice the chicken breasts into cubes and place in the slow cooker. Add the lemon juice, garlic, vinegar, olive oil, Greek yogurt, oregano, Greek seasoning, red onion, and dill to the slow cooker and stir to make sure everything is well combined.
- Cook on low for 5–6 hours or on high for 2–3 hours. In the meantime, incorporate all ingredients for the tzatziki sauce and stir. When well mixed, put in the refrigerator until the chicken is done.
- When the chicken has finished cooking, serve with pita bread and any or all of the toppings listed above.

Per serving: Calories: 245; Sodium: 543mg; Carbohydrates: 16g; Fiber: 12g; Protein: 38g

• Slow Cooker Chicken Cassoulet

Preparation Time: 10 minutes

Cooking Time: 20 minutes

Servings: 16

Ingredients

- 1 cup dry navy beans, soaked
- 8 bone-in skinless chicken thighs
- 1 Polish sausage, cooked and chopped into bite-sized pieces (optional)
- 1¼ cup tomato juice
- 1 (28-ounce) can halved tomatoes
- 1 tbsp Worcestershire sauce
- 1 tsp instant beef or chicken bouillon granules
- ½ tsp dried basil
- ½ teaspoon dried oregano
- ½ teaspoon paprika
- ½ cup chopped celery
- ½ cup chopped carrot
- ½ cup chopped onion

Directions

- Brush the slow cooker with olive oil or nonstick cooking spray. In a mixing bowl, stir together the tomato juice, tomatoes, Worcestershire sauce, beef bouillon, basil, oregano, and paprika. Make sure the ingredients are well combined.
- Place the chicken and sausage into the slow cooker and cover with the tomato juice mixture. Top with celery, carrot, and onion. Cook on low for 10–12 hours.

Per serving: Calories: 254; Sodium: 543mg; Carbohydrates: 16g; Fiber: 12g; Protein: 38g

- ## Slow Cooker Chicken Provencal

Preparation Time 5 minutes

Cooking Time: 8 hours

Servings: 4

Ingredients

- 4 (6-ounce) skinless bone-in chicken breast halves
- 2 teaspoons dried basil
- 1 teaspoon dried thyme
- 1/8 teaspoon salt
- 1/8 teaspoon freshly ground black pepper
- 1 yellow pepper, diced
- 1 red pepper, diced
- 1 (15.5-ounce) can cannellini beans
- 1 (14.5-ounce) can petite tomatoes with basil, garlic, and oregano, undrained

Directions

- Brush the slow cooker with nonstick olive oil. Add all the ingredients to the slow cooker and stir to combine. Cook on low for 8 hours.

Per serving: Calories: 111; Sodium: 543mg; Carbohydrates: 16g; Fiber: 12g; Protein: 38g

- ## Greek Style Turkey Roast

Preparation Time: 20 minutes

Cooking Time: 7 hours and 30 minutes

Servings: 8

Ingredients

- 1 (4-pound) boneless turkey breast, trimmed
- ½ cup chicken broth, divided
- 2 tablespoons fresh lemon juice
- 2 cups chopped onion

- ½ cup pitted Kalamata olives
- ½ cup oil-packed sun-dried tomatoes, thinly sliced
- 1 teaspoon Greek seasoning
- ½ teaspoon salt
- ¼ teaspoon fresh ground black pepper
- 3 tablespoons all-purpose flour (or whole wheat)

Directions

- Brush the slow cooker with nonstick cooking spray or olive oil. Add the turkey, ¼ cup of the chicken broth, lemon juice, onion, olives, sun-dried tomatoes, Greek seasoning, salt and pepper to the slow cooker.
- Cook on low for 7 hours. Scourge the flour into the remaining ¼ cup of chicken broth, then stir gently into the slow cooker. Cook for an additional 30 minutes.

Per serving: Calories: 237; Sodium: 543mg; Carbohydrates: 16g; Fiber: 12g; Protein: 38g

• Garlic Chicken with Couscous

Preparation Time: 25 minutes

Cooking Time: 7 hours

Servings: 4

Ingredients

- 1 whole chicken, cut into pieces
- 1 tablespoon extra-virgin olive oil
- 6 cloves garlic, halved
- 1 cup dry white wine
- 1 cup couscous
- ½ teaspoon salt
- ½ teaspoon pepper
- 1 medium onion, thinly sliced
- 2 teaspoons dried thyme

- 1/3 cup whole wheat flour

Directions

- Cook the olive oil in a heavy skillet. When skillet is hot, add the chicken to sear. Make sure the chicken pieces don't touch each other. Cook with the skin side down for about 3 minutes or until browned.

- Brush your slow cooker with nonstick cooking spray or olive oil. Put the onion, garlic, and thyme into the slow cooker and sprinkle with salt and pepper. Stir in the chicken on top of the onions.

- In a separate bowl, whisk the flour into the wine until there are no lumps, then pour over the chicken. Cook on low for 7 hours or until done. You can cook on high for 3 hours as well. Serve the chicken over the cooked couscous and spoon sauce over the top.

Per serving: Calories: 111; Sodium: 543mg; Carbohydrates: 16g; Fiber: 12g; Protein: 38g

• Chicken Karahi

Preparation Time: 5 minutes

Cooking Time: 5 hours

Servings: 4

Ingredients

- 2 lbs. chicken breasts or thighs
- ¼ cup olive oil
- 1 small can tomato paste
- 1 tablespoon butter
- 1 large onion, diced
- ½ cup plain Greek yogurt
- ½ cup water
- 2 tablespoons ginger in garlic paste
- 3 tablespoons fenugreek leaves
- 1 teaspoon ground coriander

- 1 medium tomato

- 1 teaspoon red chili

- 2 green chilies

- 1 teaspoon turmeric

- 1 tablespoon garam masala

- 1 teaspoon cumin powder

- 1 teaspoon sea salt

- ¼ teaspoon nutmeg

Directions

- Brush the slow cooker with nonstick cooking spray. In a small bowl, thoroughly mix together all of the spices. Mix in the chicken to the slow cooker followed by the rest of the ingredients, including the spice mixture. Stir until everything is well mixed with the spices.

- Cook on low for 4–5 hours. Serve with naan or Italian bread.

Per serving: Calories: 411; Sodium: 543mg; Carbohydrates: 16g; Fiber: 12g; Protein: 38g

- ## Chicken Cacciatore with Orzo

Preparation Time: 20 minutes

Cooking Time: 4 hours

Servings: 6

Ingredients

- 2 pounds skin-on chicken thighs

- 1 tablespoon olive oil

- 1 cup mushrooms, quartered

- 3 carrots, chopped

- 1 small jar Kalamata olives

- 2 (14-ounce) cans diced tomatoes

- 1 small can tomato paste

- 1 cup red wine
- 5 garlic cloves
- 1 cup orzo

Directions

- In a large skillet, cook the olive oil. When the oil is heated, add the chicken, skin side down, and sear it. Make sure the pieces of chicken don't touch each other.
- When the chicken is browned, add to the slow cooker along with all the ingredients except the orzo. Cook the chicken on low for 2 hours, then add the orzo and cook for an additional 2 hours. Serve with a crusty French bread.

Per serving: Calories: 345; Sodium: 543mg; Carbohydrates: 16g; Fiber: 12g; Protein: 38g

Meat

- ## Squash Soup with Peppers

Preparation Time: 15 minutes

Cooking Time: 20 minutes

Servings: 2

Ingredients:

- ½ lb. butternut squash, chunks
- 1 cup kale, torn
- 1 red bell pepper, chopped
- 1 cup yellow bell pepper, chopped
- 5-6 green pitted olives
- 2 stalks celery, chopped
- 4 cups water
- 1 tsp. oregano
- 1 tsp. Dijon mustard
- Pinch of salt and white pepper

Directions:

- Boil 4 cups of water in a large saucepan. Lower the heat to medium.
- Add the cubed squash, chopped bell peppers, kale, celery, olives, salt and spices.
- Cover with the lid and let the soup simmer for 15 minutes. Cool and blend to a smooth paste.
- Top with chopped parsley leaves, spring onion, seeds, or nuts. Serve hot with toasted bread, baked nachos, or crackers.

Per serving: Calories: 101; Sodium: 543mg; Carbohydrates: 16g; Fiber: 12g; Protein: 38g

- # Grilled Steak, Mushroom and Onion Kebabs

Preparation Time: 10 minutes

Cooking Time: 10 minutes

Servings: 2

Ingredients:

- 1 lb. boneless top sirloin steak
- 8 oz. white button mushrooms
- 1 medium red onion
- 4 peeled garlic cloves
- 2 rosemary sprigs
- 2 tsps. extra-virgin olive oil
- ¼ tsp. black pepper.
- 2 tsps. red wine vinegar
- ¼ tsp. sea salt

Directions:

- Soak 12 (10-inch) wooden skewers in water. Spray the cold grill with nonstick cooking spray and heat the grill to medium-high.
- Cut a piece of aluminum foil into a 10-inch square. Place the garlic and rosemary sprigs in the center, drizzle with 1 tbsp. of oil and wrap tightly to form a foil packet.
- Arrange it on the grill and seal the grill cover.
- Cut the steak into 1-inch cubes. Thread the beef onto the wet skewers, alternating with whole mushrooms and onion wedges. Spray the kebabs thoroughly with nonstick cooking spray and sprinkle with pepper.
- Cook the kebabs on the covered grill for 5 minutes.
- Flip and grill for 5 more minutes while covered.
- Unwrap foil packets with garlic and rosemary sprigs and put them into a small bowl.
- Carefully strip the rosemary sprigs of their leaves into the bowl and pour in any accumulated juices and oil from the foil packet.

- Mix in the remaining 1 tbsp. of oil and the vinegar and salt.
- Mash the garlic with a fork, and mix all the ingredients in the bowl together. Pour over the finished steak kebabs and serve.

Per serving: Calories: 111; Sodium: 543mg; Carbohydrates: 16g; Fiber: 12g; Protein: 38g

• Mediterranean Lamb Chops

Preparation Time: 10 minutes

Cooking Time: 20 minutes

Servings: 2

Ingredients:

- 4 lamb shoulder chops, 8 oz. each
- 2 tbsps. Dijon mustard
- 2 tbsps. Balsamic vinegar
- 1 tbsp. garlic, chopped
- ½ cup olive oil
- 2 tbsps. shredded fresh basil
- Pepper

Directions:

- Pat your lamb chop dry using a kitchen towel and arrange them on a shallow glass baking dish.
- Take a bowl and whisk in Dijon mustard, balsamic vinegar, garlic, pepper, and mix them well.
- Whisk in the oil very slowly into the marinade until the mixture is smooth.
- Stir in the basil.
- Pour the marinade over the lamb chops and stir to coat both sides well.
- Cover the chops and allow them to marinate for 1-4 hours (chilled).
- Take the chops out and leave them for 30 minutes to allow the temperature to reach the normal level.
- Preheat your grill to medium heat and add oil to the grate.

- Grill the lamb chops for 5-10 minutes per side until both sides are browned.
- Once the center of the chop reads 145°F, the chops are ready, serve it and enjoy!

Per serving: Calories: 111; Sodium: 543mg; Carbohydrates: 16g; Fiber: 12g; Protein: 38g

• Oven Roasted Garlic Chicken Thigh

Preparation Time: 10 minutes

Cooking Time: 55 minutes

Servings: 2

Ingredients:

- 8 chicken thighs
- Salt and pepper as needed
- 1 tbsp. extra-virgin olive oil
- 6 garlic cloves, peeled and crushed
- 1 jar (10 oz.) roasted red peppers, drained and chopped
- 1½ lbs. potatoes, diced
- 2 cups cherry tomatoes, halved
- 1/3 cup capers, sliced
- 1 tsp. dried Italian seasoning
- 1 tbsp. fresh basil

Directions:

- Season the chicken with kosher salt and black pepper.
- Take a cast-iron skillet over medium-high heat and heat up olive oil.
- Sear the chicken on both sides.
- Add the remaining ingredients except for basil and stir well.
- Remove the heat and place a cast-iron skillet in the oven.
- Bake for 45 minutes at 400°F until the internal temperature reaches 165°F.
- Serve it and enjoy!

Per serving: Calories: 386; Sodium: 543mg; Carbohydrates: 16g; Fiber: 12g; Protein: 38g

• Balearic Beef Brisket Bowl

Preparation Time: 0 minutes

Cooking Time: 50 minutes

Servings: 2

Ingredients:

- ½ cup Manto Negro dry red wine (Spanish or Mallorca dry red wine)
- 1/3 cup olives, pitted and chopped
- 14.5 oz. tomatoes with juice (diced)
- 5 garlic cloves, chopped
- ½ tsp. dried rosemary
- Salt and pepper
- 2½ lbs. beef brisket
- Olive oil
- 1 tbsp. fresh parsley, finely chopped
- 1½ cups sautéed green
- beans

Directions:

- Pour the dry wine and olives into your slow cooker and stir in the tomatoes, garlic and rosemary.
- Sprinkle salt and pepper to taste over the beef brisket. Place the seasoned meat on top of the wine-tomato mixture. Ladle half of the mixture over the meat. Cover the slow cooker and cook for 6 hours on High heat until fork-tender.
- Transfer the cooked brisket to a chopping board. Tent the meat with foil and let it stand for 10 minutes.
- Drizzle with olive oil. Cut the brisket into 6-slices across its grain. Transfer the slices to a serving platter and spoon some sauce over the meat slices. Sprinkle with parsley.

- Serve with sautéed green beans and the remaining sauce.

Per serving: Calories: 111; Sodium: 543mg; Carbohydrates: 16g; Fiber: 12g; Protein: 38g

• Chicken Marsala

Preparation Time: 10 minutes

Cooking Time: 45 minutes

Servings: 2

Ingredients:

- 2 tbsps. olive oil
- 4 skinless, boneless chicken breast cutlets
- ¾ tbsp. black pepper, divided
- ½ tsp. kosher salt, divided
- 8 oz. mushrooms, sliced
- 4 thyme sprigs
- 0.2 quarts unsalted chicken stock
- ½ quarts Marsala wine
- tbsps. olive oil
- tbsp. fresh thyme, chopped

Directions:

- Heat oil in a pan and fry the chicken for 4-5 minutes per side. Remove the chicken from the pan and set it aside.
- In the same pan, add thyme, mushrooms, salt and pepper; stir fry for 1-2 minutes.
- Add Marsala wine, chicken broth and cooked chicken. Let it simmer for 10-12 minutes on low heat.
- Add to a serving dish.
- Enjoy.

Per serving: Calories: 356; Sodium: 543mg; Carbohydrates: 16g; Fiber: 12g; Protein: 38g

- ## Herb Roasted Chicken

Preparation Time: 20 minutes

Cooking Time: 45 minutes

Servings: 2

Ingredients:

- 1 tbsp. virgin olive oil
- 1 whole chicken
- 2 rosemary springs
- 3 garlic cloves (peeled)
- 1 lemon (cut in half)
- 1 tsp. sea salt
- 1 tsp. black pepper

Directions:

- Turn your oven to 450°F.
- Take your whole chicken and pat it dry using paper towels. Then rub in the olive oil. Remove the leaves from 1 of the springs of rosemary and scatter them over the chicken. Sprinkle the sea salt and black pepper over the top. Place the other whole sprig of rosemary into the cavity of the chicken. Then add in the garlic cloves and lemon halves.
- Place the chicken into a roasting pan and then place it into the oven. Allow the chicken to bake for 1 hour, check that the internal temperature should be at least 165°F. If the chicken begins to brown too much, cover it with foil and return it to the oven to finish cooking.
- When the chicken has cooked to the appropriate temperature, remove it from the oven. Let it rest for at least 20 minutes before carving.
- Serve with a large side of roasted or steamed vegetables or your favorite salad.

Per serving: Calories: 111; Sodium: 543mg; Carbohydrates: 16g; Fiber: 12g; Protein: 38g

• Grilled Harissa Chicken

Preparation Time: 20 minutes

Cooking Time: 12 minutes

Servings: 2

Ingredients:

- 1 lemon juice
- ½ sliced red onion
- 1½ tsps. coriander
- 1½ tsps. smoked paprika
- 1 tsp. cumin
- 2 tsps. cayenne
- Olive oil
- 1½ tsps. black pepper
- Kosher salt
- 8 boneless chickens.

Directions:

- Get a large bowl. Season your chicken with kosher salt on all sides, then add the onions, garlic, lemon juice and harissa paste to the bowl.
- Add about 3 tablespoons of olive oil to the mixture. Heat a grill to 459 heats (an indoor or outdoor grill works just fine), then oil the grates.
- Grill each side of the chicken for about 7 minutes. Its temperature should register 165°F on a thermometer and it should be fully cooked by then.

Per serving: Calories: 387; Sodium: 543mg; Carbohydrates: 16g; Fiber: 12g; Protein: 38g

• Turkish Turkey Mini Meatloaves

Preparation Time: 15 minutes

Cooking Time: 20 minutes

Servings: 2

Ingredients:

- 1 lb. ground turkey breast
- 1 egg
- ¼ cup whole-wheat breadcrumbs, crushed
- ¼ cup feta cheese, plus more for topping
- ¼ cup Kalamata olives halved
- ¼ cup fresh parsley, chopped
- ¼ cup red onion, minced
- ¼ cup + 2 tbsps. hummus
- 2 garlic cloves, minced
- ½ tsp. dried basil
- ¼ tsp. dried oregano
- Salt and pepper
- ½ small cucumber, peeled, seeded, and chopped
- 1 large tomato, chopped
- 3 tbsps. fresh basil, chopped
- ½-lemon juice
- 1 tsp. extra-virgin olive oil
- Salt and pepper

Directions:

- Preheat your oven to 425 °F.
- Line a 5"x9" baking sheet with foil and spray the surfaces with non-stick grease. Set it aside.
- Except for the ¼ cup of hummus, combine and mix all the turkey meatloaf ingredients in a large mixing bowl. Mix well until fully combined.

- Divide the mixture equally into 4 portions. Form the portions into loaves. Spread a tablespoon of the remaining hummus on each meatloaf. Place the loaves on the greased baking sheet.

- Bake for 20 minutes until the loaves no longer appear pink in the center (Ensure the meatloaf cooks through by inserting a meat thermometer and the reading reaches 165 ⁰F).

- Combine and mix all the topping ingredients in a small mixing bowl. Mix well until fully combined.

- To serve, spoon the topping over the cooked meatloaves.

Per serving: Calories: 233; Sodium: 543mg; Carbohydrates: 16g; Fiber: 12g; Protein: 38g

• Lemon Caper Chicken

Preparation Time: 10 minutes

Cooking Time: 15 minutes

Servings: 2

Ingredients:

- 2 tbsps. virgin olive oil
- 2 chicken breasts (boneless, skinless, cut in half, lb. to ¾ an inch thick)
- ¼ cup capers
- 2 lemons (wedges)
- 1 tsp. oregano
- 1 tsp. basil
- ½ tsp. black pepper

Directions:

- Take a large skillet and place it on your stove and add the olive oil to it. Turn the heat to medium and allow it to warm up.

- As the oil heats up, season your chicken breast with the oregano, basil and black pepper on each side.

- Place your chicken breast into the hot skillet and cook on each side for 5 minutes.
- Transfer the chicken from the skillet to your dinner plate. Top with capers and serve with a few lemon wedges.

Per serving: Calories: 345; Sodium: 543mg; Carbohydrates: 16g; Fiber: 12g; Protein: 38g

• Buttery Garlic Chicken

Preparation Time: 5 minutes

Cooking Time: 40 minutes

Servings: 2

Ingredients:

- 2 tbsps. ghee, melted
- 2 boneless skinless chicken breasts
- 1 tbsp. dried Italian seasoning
- 4 tbsps. butter
- ¼ cup grated Parmesan cheese
- Himalayan salt and pepper

Directions:

- Preheat the oven to 375°F. Select a baking dish that fits both chicken breasts and coat it with ghee.
- Pat dries the chicken breasts. Season with pink Himalayan salt, pepper, and Italian seasoning. Place the chicken in the baking dish.
- In a medium skillet over medium heat, melt the butter. Sauté the minced garlic, for about 5 minutes.
- Remove the butter-garlic mixture from the heat and pour it over the chicken breasts.
- Roast in the oven for 30 to 35 minutes. Sprinkle some of the Parmesan cheese on top of each chicken breast. Let the chicken rest in the baking dish for 5 minutes.
- Divide the chicken between 2 plates; spoon the butter sauce over the chicken and serve it.

Per serving: Calories: 111; Sodium: 543mg; Carbohydrates: 16g; Fiber: 12g; Protein: 38g

• Creamy Chicken-Spinach Skillet

Preparation Time: 10 minutes

Cooking Time: 17 minutes

Servings: 2

Ingredients:

- 1 lb. boneless skinless chicken breast
- 1 medium diced onion
- 12 oz. diced roasted red peppers
- 2 ½ cup chicken stock
- 2 cups baby spinach leaves
- 2 ½ tsp. butter
- 4 minced garlic cloves
- 7 oz. cream cheese
- Salt and pepper, to taste

Directions:

- Place a saucepan on medium-high heat for 2 minutes. Add the butter and melt it for a minute, swirling to coat the pan.
- Add the chicken to a pan, season with pepper and salt to taste. Cook the chicken on high heat for 3 minutes per side.
- Lower the heat to medium and stir in the onions, red peppers and garlic. Sauté for 5 minutes and deglaze the pot with a little bit of stock.
- Whisk in the chicken stock and cream cheese. Cook and mix until thoroughly combined.
- Stir in the spinach and adjust the seasoning to taste. Cook for 2 minutes or until the spinach is wilted.
- Serve it and enjoy.

Per serving: Calories: 111; Sodium: 543mg; Carbohydrates: 16g; Fiber: 12g; Protein: 38g

- ## Slow Cooker Meatloaf

Preparation Time: 10 minutes

Cooking Time: 6 hours and 10 minutes

Servings: 2

Ingredients:

- 2 lbs. ground bison
- 1 grated zucchini
- 2 large eggs
- Olive oil cooking spray as required
- 1 zucchini, shredded
- ½ cup parsley, fresh, finely chopped
- ½ cup parmesan cheese, shredded
- 3 tbsps. Balsamic vinegar
- 4 garlic cloves, grated
- 2 tbsps. Onion minced
- 1 tbsp. Dried oregano
- ½ tsp. Ground black pepper
- ½ tsp. Kosher salt

For the topping:

- ¼ cup shredded mozzarella cheese
- ¼ cup ketchup without sugar
- ¼ cup fresh chopped parsley

Directions:

- Stripe line the inside of a 6-quart slow cooker with aluminum foil. Spray non-stick cooking oil over it.
- In a large bowl, combine ground bison or extra-lean ground sirloin, zucchini, eggs, parsley, balsamic vinegar, garlic, dried oregano, sea or kosher salt, minced dry onion and ground black pepper.
- Situate this mixture into the slow cooker and form an oblong-shaped loaf. Cover the cooker, set on low heat and cook for 6 hours. After cooking, open the cooker and spread ketchup all over the meatloaf.
- Now, place the cheese above the ketchup as a new layer and close the slow cooker. Let the meatloaf sit on these 2 layers for about 10 minutes or until the cheese starts to melt. Garnish it with fresh parsley and shredded Mozzarella cheese.

Per serving: Calories: 111; Sodium: 543mg; Carbohydrates: 16g; Fiber: 12g; Protein: 38g

• Mediterranean Bowl

Preparation Time: 25 minutes

Cooking Time: 30 minutes

Servings: 2

Ingredients:

- 2 chicken breasts (chopped into 4 halves)
- 2 diced onions
- 2 bottles of lemon pepper marinade
- 2 diced green bell pepper
- 4 lemon juices
- 8 cloves of crushed garlic.
- 5 tsps. olive oil
- Feta cheese
- 1 grape tomato

- 1 large-sized diced zucchini and 1 small-sized. Otherwise, use 2 medium-sized diced zucchinis.
- Salt and pepper (according to your desired taste), 4 cups of water.
- Kalamata olives (as much as you fancy)
- 1 cup of garbanzo beans

Directions:

- Cook the chicken breasts in boiling water for 20 minutes.
- Sauté the onion, diced bell pepper, 1 teaspoon of garlic, olive oil and ½ lemon juice and a cup of water in a medium-sized pot for 8 minutes on medium heat.
- After 8 minutes, add your diced chicken breast into the pot and cook for 2 more minutes on medium heat (Leave the rest of the cooking to your preferred choice).
- Serve with feta cheese (as much as you like), ½ teaspoon of lemon pepper marinade and 1 sliced tomato on top followed by a cup of cooked garbanzo beans.
- Serve it with 1 sliced zucchini and diced olives of your choice!

Per serving: Calories: 111; Sodium: 543mg; Carbohydrates: 16g; Fiber: 12g; Protein: 38g

- **Tasty Lamb Leg**

Preparation Time: 10 minutes

Cooking Time: 20 minutes

Servings: 2

Ingredients:

- 2 lbs. leg of lamb, boneless and cut into chunks
- 1 tbsp. olive oil
- 1 tbsp. garlic, sliced
- 1 cup red wine
- 1 cup onion, chopped
- 2 carrots, chopped
- 1 tsp. rosemary, chopped
- 2 tsps. thyme, chopped

- 1 tsp. oregano, chopped
- ½ cup beef stock
- 2 tbsps. tomato paste
- Pepper
- Salt

Directions:

- Put oil into the inner pot of the instant pot and set the pot on sauté mode.
- Add the meat and sauté until browned.
- Add the remaining ingredients and stir well.
- Seal the pot with the lid and cook on High for 15 minutes.
- Once done, allow to release the pressure naturally. Remove the lid.
- Stir well and serve it.

Per serving: Calories: 111; Sodium: 543mg; Carbohydrates: 16g; Fiber: 12g; Protein: 38g

• Mediterranean Beef Skewers

Preparation Time: 5 minutes

Cooking Time: 8 minutes

Servings: 2

Ingredients:

- 2 lbs. cubed beef sirloin.
- 3 minced garlic cloves
- 1 tbsp. fresh lemon zest
- 1 tbsp. chopped parsley
- 2 tsps. chopped thyme
- 2 tsps. minced rosemary
- 2 tsps. dried oregano
- 4 tsps. olive oil
- 2 tsps. fresh lemon juice

- Sea salt and ground black pepper

Directions:

- Add all the ingredients, except the beef, to a bowl.
- Preheat the grill to medium-high heat.
- Mix in the beef to marinate for 1 hour.
- Arrange the marinated beef onto skewers, then cook on the preheated grill for 8 minutes, flipping occasionally.
- Once cooked, leave it aside to rest for 5 minutes; then serve it.

Per serving: Calories: 345; Sodium: 543mg; Carbohydrates: 16g; Fiber: 12g; Protein: 38g

- ## Turkey Meatballs

Preparation Time: 10 minutes

Cooking Time: 25 minutes

Servings: 2

Ingredients:

- ¼ diced yellow onion
- 14 oz. diced artichoke hearts
- 1 lb. ground turkey
- 1 tsp. dried parsley
- 1 tsp. oil
- 4 tsps. chopped basil.
- Pepper and salt, to taste.

Directions:

- Grease the baking sheet and preheat the oven to 350°F.
- On medium heat, place a nonstick medium saucepan, sauté the artichoke hearts and diced onions for 5 minutes or until onions are soft.

- Meanwhile, in a big bowl, mix the parsley, basil and ground turkey with your hands. Season to taste.
- When the onion mixture has cooled, add it into the bowl and mix thoroughly.
- With an ice cream scooper, scoop ground turkey and form balls.
- Place on a prepared cooking sheet, pop in the oven and bake until cooked around 15-20 minutes.
- Remove it from the pan. Serve it and enjoy.

Per serving: Calories: 111; Sodium: 543mg; Carbohydrates: 16g; Fiber: 12g; Protein: 38g

• Mushroom and Beef Risotto

Preparation Time: 5 minutes

Cooking Time: 10 minutes

Servings: 2

Ingredients:

- 2 cups low-sodium beef stock
- 2 cups water
- 2 tbsps. olive oil
- ½ cup scallions, chopped
- 1 cup Arborio rice
- 1 cup roast beef, thinly stripped
- ½ cup canned cream of mushroom
- Salt and pepper as needed
- Oregano, chopped
- Parsley, chopped

Directions:

- Take a stockpot and put it over medium heat.
- Add water with beef stock in it.
- Take the mixture to a boil and remove the heat.

- Take another heavy-bottomed saucepan and put it over medium heat.
- Add in the scallions and stir fry them for 1 minute.
- Add in the rice and cook it for at least 2 minutes, occasionally stirring it to ensure that it is finely coated with oil.
- In the rice mixture, keep adding your beef stock, ½ cup at a time, making sure to stir it often.
- When all the stock has been included, cook the rice for another 2 minutes.
- During the last 5 minutes of your cooking, make sure to add the beef, cream of the mushroom while stirring it nicely.
- Transfer the whole mix to a serving dish.
- Garnish with some chopped-up parsley and oregano. Serve it hot.

Per serving: Calories: 362; Sodium: 543mg; Carbohydrates: 16g; Fiber: 12g; Protein: 38g

Side Dishes

- ## Garlic Prawns with Tomatoes and Basil

Preparation Time: 10 minutes

Cooking Time: 10 minutes

Servings: 2

Ingredients:

- 2 tsps. olive oil
- 1¼ lbs. prawns peeled and deveined
- 3 garlic cloves minced
- 1/8 tsp. crushed red pepper flakes
- ¾ cup dry white wine
- 1½ cups grape tomatoes
- ¼ cup finely chopped fresh basil plus more for garnish
- ¾ tsp. salt
- ½ tsp. ground black pepper

  Directions:

- In a skillet, heat the oil over medium-high heat. Add the prawns and cook for 1 minute, or until just cooked through. Transfer to a plate.
- Add the red pepper flakes and garlic to the oil in the pan and cook, stirring for 30 seconds. Stir in the wine and cook until it's reduced by about half.
- Add the tomatoes and stir-fry until the tomatoes begin to break down (about 3 to 4 minutes). Stir in the reserved shrimp, salt, pepper and basil. Cook for 1 to 2 more minutes.
- Serve it garnished with the remaining basil.

Per serving: Calories: 111; Sodium: 543mg; Carbohydrates: 16g; Fiber: 12g; Protein: 38g

• Stuffed Calamari in Tomato Sauce

Preparation Time: 10 minutes

Cooking Time: 25 minutes

Servings: 2

Ingredients:

- ½ cup olive oil plus 3 tbsps. divided
- 2 large onions finely chopped
- 4 garlic cloves finely chopped
- Grated Pecorino Romano—1 cup Grated Pecorino Romano plus ¼ cup, divided
- ½ cup chopped flat-leaf parsley plus ¼ cup, divided
- 6 cups breadcrumbs
- 1 cup raisins
- 12 cleaned large squid tubes
- 12 toothpicks

    For the Tomato Sauce:

- 2 tsps. olive oil
- 4 garlic cloves chopped
- 2 (28-oz.) crushed tomatoes cans
- ½ cup finely chopped basil
- 1 tsp. salt
- 1 tsp. pepper

    Directions:

- Combine the saffron threads with 2 tablespoons of warm water.
- In a Dutch oven, heat ½ cup of olive oil. Add the onions and ½ tsp. of salt and stir-fry for 5 minutes. Add the tomato paste and cook for 1 minute more.
- Add the wine and bring it to a boil. Add the fish broth and soaked saffron and bring back to a boil. Lower the heat to low and simmer, uncovered, for 10 minutes.

- Meanwhile, in a food processor, combine the bread and garlic and process until ground.
- Add the remaining ¼ cup of olive oil and ½ teaspoon of salt and pulse just to mix.
- Add the fish to the pot; cover and cook until the fish is just cooked through about 6 minutes. Stir in the sauce. Taste and adjust the seasoning.
- Ladle the stew into the serving bowls.
- Serve it garnished with parsley.

Per serving: Calories: 111; Sodium: 543mg; Carbohydrates: 16g; Fiber: 12g; Protein: 38g

- ## Provencal Braised Hake

Preparation Time: 10 minutes

Cooking Time: 20 minutes

Servings: 2

Ingredients:

- 2 tbsps. extra-virgin olive oil plus extra for serving
- 1 onion halved and sliced thin
- 1 fennel bulb stalks discarded, bulb halved, cored, and sliced thin
- Salt and black pepper
- 4 garlic cloves minced
- 1 tsp. minced fresh thyme
- 1 (14.5 oz.) diced tomatoes can be drained
- ½ cup dry white wine
- 4 (4 to 6 oz.) 1 to 1½-inch thick skinless hake fillets
- 2 tsps. minced fresh parsley

Directions:

- Heat the oil in a skillet over medium heat. Add the fennel, onion and ½ tsp. of salt and cook for 5 minutes. Stir in the thyme and garlic and cook for 30 seconds.
- Stir in the wine and tomatoes and then bring to a simmer.

- Pat the hake dry with paper towels and season with salt and pepper. Place the hake into the skillet (skin side down). Spoon some sauce over the top and bring to a simmer.
- Lower the heat to medium-low, cover and cook for 10 to 12 minutes, or until the hake flakes apart when prodded with a knife.
- Serve the hake into individual bowls. Stir parsley into the sauce and season with salt and pepper to taste. Spoon the sauce over the hake and drizzle with extra oil.
- Serve it.

Per serving: Calories: 111; Sodium: 543mg; Carbohydrates: 16g; Fiber: 12g; Protein: 38g

• **Pan-Roasted Sea Bass**

Preparation Time: 5 minutes

Cooking Time: 10 minutes

Servings: 2

Ingredients:

- 4 (4 to 6 oz.) 1 to 1½ skinless sea bass fillets inches thick
- Salt and pepper
- ½ tsp. sugar
- 1 tsp. extra-virgin olive oil
- Lemon wedges

  Directions:

- Place the oven rack in the middle and preheat the oven to 425°F. Pat the sea bass dry with paper towels and season with salt and pepper. On 1 side of each fillet, sprinkle the sugar evenly.
- In a skillet, heat the oil over medium-high. Place the sea bass sugared side down in the skillet and cook for 2 minutes, or until browned.
- Then flip and transfer the skillet to the oven and roast for 7 to 10 minutes, or until the fish registers 145°F.

- Serve it with lemon wedges.

Per serving: Calories: 111; Sodium: 543mg; Carbohydrates: 16g; Fiber: 12g; Protein: 38g

• Vegetarian Paella with Green Beans and Chickpeas

Preparation Time: 10 minutes

Cooking Time: 35 minutes

Servings: 2

Ingredients:

- Pinch of saffron
- 3 cups vegetable broth
- 1 tsp. olive oil
- 1 large yellow onion diced
- 4 garlic cloves sliced
- 1 red bell pepper diced
- ¾ cup crushed tomatoes fresh or canned
- 2 tsps. tomato paste
- 1½ tsps. hot paprika
- 1 tsp. salt
- ½ tsp. freshly ground black pepper
- 1½ cups green beans trimmed and halved
- 1 (15-oz.) chickpeas can, drained and rinsed
- 1 cup short-grain white rice
- 1 lemon cut into wedges

  Directions:

- Mix the saffron threads with 3 tablespoons of warm water in a small bowl.
- In a saucepan, bring the water to a simmer over medium heat. Lower the heat to low and let the broth simmer.

- Heat the oil in a skillet over medium heat. Add the onion and stir-fry for 5 minutes.
- Add the bell pepper and garlic and stir-fry for 7 minutes or until the pepper is softened.
- Stir in the saffron-water mixture, salt, pepper, paprika, tomato paste and tomatoes.
- Add the rice, chickpeas and green beans. Add the warm broth and bring to a boil.
- Lower the heat and simmer uncovered for 20 minutes.
- Serve it hot, garnished with lemon wedges.

Per serving: Calories: 111; Sodium: 543mg; Carbohydrates: 16g; Fiber: 12g; Protein: 38g

• Speedy Sweet Potato Chips

Preparation Time: 15 minutes

Cooking Time: 1 hour

Servings: 2

Ingredients:

- 1 large sweet potato
- 1 tbsp. extra virgin olive oil
- Salt

   Directions:

- Preheat the oven to 300°F. Slice your potato into nice, thin slices that resemble fries.
- Toss the potato slices with salt and extra virgin olive oil in a bowl. Bake for about 1 hour, flipping every 15 minutes until crispy and browned.

Per serving: Calories: 111; Sodium: 543mg; Carbohydrates: 16g; Fiber: 12g; Protein: 38g

- ## Classic Apple Oats

Preparation Time: 10 minutes

Cooking Time: 15 minutes

Servings: 2

Ingredients:

- ½ tsp. cinnamon
- ¼ tsp. ginger
- 2 apples make half-inch chunks
- ½ cup oats, steel-cut
- 1½ cups of water
- Maple syrup
- ¼ tsp. salt
- Clove
- ¼ tsp. nutmeg

Directions:

- Take Instant Pot and careful y arrange it over a clean, dry kitchen platform.
- Turn on the appliance.
- In the cooking pot area, add the water, oats, cinnamon, ginger, clove, nutmeg, apple, and salt. Stir the ingredients gently.
- Close the pot lid and seal the valve to avoid any leakage. Find and press the "Manual" cooking setting and set the cooking time to 5 minutes.
- Allow the recipe ingredients to cook for the set time, and after that, the timer reads "zero."
- Press "Cancel" and press the "NPR" setting for natural pressure release. It takes 8-10 times for all inside pressure to release.
- Open the pot and arrange the cooked recipe on serving plates.
- Sweeten as needed with maple or agave syrup and serve immediately.
- Top with some chopped nuts, optional.

Per serving: Calories: 111; Sodium: 543mg; Carbohydrates: 16g; Fiber: 12g; Protein: 38g

• Peach and Chia Seed

Preparation Time: 10 minutes

Cooking Time: 10 minutes

Servngs: 2

Ingredients:

- ½ oz. chia seeds
- 1 tbsp. pure maple syrup
- 1 cup coconut milk
- 1 tsp. ground cinnamon
- 3 diced peaches
- 2/3 cups granola

   Directions:

- Find a small bowl and add the chia seeds, maple syrup and coconut milk.
- Stir well, then cover and pop into the fridge for at least 1 hour.
- Find another bowl, add the peaches and sprinkle with the cinnamon. Pop to one side.
- When it's time to serve, take 2 glasses and pour the chia mixture between the 2.
- Sprinkle the granola over the top, keeping a tiny amount to 1 side to use to decorate later.
- Top with the peaches and top with the reserved granola and serve it.

Per serving: Calories: 289; Sodium: 543mg; Carbohydrates: 16g; Fiber: 12g; Protein: 38g

• Avocado Spread

Preparation Time: 10 minutes

Cooking Time: 1 minute

Servings: 2

Ingredients:

- 2 peeled and pitted avocados
- 1 tbsp. olive oil
- 1 tbsp. minced shallots
- 1 tbsp. lime juice
- 1 tbsp. heavy coconut cream
- Salt
- Black pepper
- 1 tbsp. chopped chives

Directions:

- In a blender, combine the avocado flesh with the oil, shallots and the other ingredients, except for the chopped chives.
- Pulse well; divide into bowls. Sprinkle the chives on top and serve as a morning spread.

Per serving: Calories: 111; Sodium: 543mg; Carbohydrates: 16g; Fiber: 12g; Protein: 38g

• Almond Butter and Blueberry Smoothie

Preparation Time: 10 minutes

Cooking Time: 1 minute

Servings: 2

Ingredients:

- 1 cup almond milk
- 1 cup blueberries
- 4 ice cubes
- 1 scoop vanilla protein powder
- 1 tbsp. almond butter
- 1 tbsp. chia seeds

Directions:

- Use a blender to mix the almond butter, vanilla protein powder, chia seeds, almond milk, ice cubes and blueberries together until the consistency is smooth.

Per servings: Calories: 456; Sodium: 543mg; Carbohydrates: 16g; Fiber: 12g; Protein: 38g

• Salmon and Egg Muffins

Preparation Time: 10 minutes

Cooking Time: 15 minutes

Servings: 2

Ingredients:

- 4 eggs
- 1/3 cup milk
- Salt and pepper
- 1½ oz. smoked salmon
- 1 tbsp. chopped chives
- Green onions, optional

Directions:

- Preheat the oven to 356°F and grease 6 muffin tin holes with a small amount of olive oil.
- Place the eggs, milk and a pinch of salt and pepper into a small bowl and lightly beat to combine.
- Divide the egg mixture between the 6 muffin holes; then divide the salmon between the muffins and place into each hole, gently pressing down to submerge in the egg mixture, chopped.
- Sprinkle each muffin with chopped chives and place in the oven for about 8-10 minutes or until just set.
- Leave to cool for about 5 minutes before turning out and storing it in an airtight container in the fridge.

   Per servings: Calories: 345; Sodium: 543mg; Carbohydrates: 16g; Fiber: 12g; Protein: 38g

- ## Nachos

Preparation Time: 5 minutes

Cooking Time: 10 minutes

Servings: 2

Ingredients:

- 2 oz. restaurant-style corn tortilla chips
- ½ medium green onion, thinly sliced (about 1 tsp.)
- 1 (2 oz.) package finely crumbled feta cheese
- ½ finely chopped and drained plum tomato
- 1 tbsp. Sun-dried tomatoes in oil, finely chopped
- 1 tbsp. Kalamata olives

Directions:

- Mix an onion, plum tomato, oil, sun-dried tomatoes and olives in a small bowl.
- Arrange the tortillas chips on a microwavable plate in a single layer topped evenly with cheese—microwave on high for 1 minute.
- Rotate the plate half turn and continue microwaving until the cheese is bubbly. Spread the tomato mixture over the chips and cheese and enjoy.

Per servings: Calories: 245; Sodium: 543mg; Carbohydrates: 16g; Fiber: 12g; Protein: 38g

Conclusion

The benefits of the Mediterranean diet have been thoroughly researched in the past, with an emphasis on cardiovascular disease and obesity. The adavantages of a Mediterranean diet are well established, but whether they actually improve general health or just lower risk factors is still up for debate. According to a new meta-analysis that was published in the Annals of Internal Medicine, eating a Mediterranean-style diet lowers the risk of heart attacks by 22%. Additionally, it was discovered that when compared to low-fat diets like the Atkins, diets high in fruits, vegetables, nuts, and unprocessed food lowered all cause mortality by 12%. This study expanded on earlier extensive meta analyses that showed a 20% decrease in heart disease risk after adhering to this type of diet for ten years. Although smaller studies have suggested that eating a Mediterranean-style diet can reduce cancer risk by up to 30%, the Mediterranean diet is not linked to an increased risk of the disease. The larger cancer risk reduction is explained by the Mediterranean diet's tendency to encourage consumption of more red meat, saturated fat, and sodium. An increased risk of breast cancer has been linked to these higher consumption. This most recent meta-analysis confirmed earlier studies on the advantages of the Mediterranean diet, but it left open certain important issues. Vegan diets were not examined in the study, nor was it determined whether they offered the same advantages as a high consumption of vegetables, fruits, and olive oil. How much of the Mediterranean Diet's health benefits are genuinely dependent on the caliber of the food ingested is another crucial topic. Plant-based diets frequently include supplements, however these can impair the body's capacity to absorb vitamins and minerals for optimum health. This study found that eating a Mediterranean-style diet helped lower all-cause mortality by 12%, but it failed to take these lifestyle variations into account.

The fundamental distinction between the Mediterranean Diet and other well-known diets is that the former forgoes foods heavy in cholesterol, salt, and saturated fat. It also emphasizes consuming more whole grains, vegetables, fruit, nuts, and other naturally occurring carbs. A high intake of omega-3 fatty acids and a diet low in meat are thought to lower the risk of heart disease. Vegetables, fruits, legumes, whole grains, fish, and healthy fats such as virgin olive oil are abundant in the traditional Mediterranean diet. Moderate red wine consumption is another component of the traditional diet. Due of its high sugar content, wine has been eliminated from the modern understanding of this diet.

When compared to other diets like low-carb, high-protein diets or the Atkins eating plan, the Mediterranean Diet consumes less red meat and saturated fat. Because of this, a lower all-cause mortality has been linked to the Mediterranean diet. In terms of the risk of cardiovascular disease, there are also no appreciable differences between the Mediterranean Diet and other high protein, low cholesterol, low saturated fat diets. There is some evidence to support why the Mediterranean diet is beneficial, even though there is no data to support that it will reduce cancer or total mortality.

Made in United States
Troutdale, OR
01/12/2024

16905935R00071